the pet *ferret* owner's manual

written by
JUDITH A. BELL, DVM, PhD

To my friend Dean Manning,
and to the memories of
Miracle, Dana and Georgina, three
very special ferrets
we built from scratch.

Miracle

This book will give you information on caring for your new ferret whether it is a baby purchased at a pet shop or an adult acquired from a shelter or a private breeder. It assumes that you have never had a ferret before and know nothing about them. Even if you've had ferrets for years, you may learn things you wondered about but didn't know who to ask. When the text seems very rudimentary, there are references to more detailed information located elsewhere in the book.

Text: © Judith A. Bell, DVM, PhD 1995
Design by Christopher Maggio Studio, Inc.
Photography: © Christopher Maggio 1995
Eye and cataract photographs supplied by Dr. Paul Miller,
School of Veterinary Medicine, University of Wisconsin-Madison.
Author's portrait taken by Dean Manning.

ISBN: 0-9646477-2-9 PB
0-9646477-1-0 LB

The Pet Ferret Owner's Manual first published in the United States of America by: Christopher Maggio Studio, Inc. and Miracle Workers, Rochester, New York, U.S.A.

table of contents

Chapter 1: Introducing the Domestic Ferret   6
What is a ferret?   6
Who owns ferrets?   6
Where do ferrets come from - are there any wild ones?   6
Coat colors   7
How long do ferrets live?   8
How much care does a ferret need?   8

Chapter 2: Benefits and Costs of Ferret Ownership   9
Ferrets make good pets   9
What do people like about ferrets?   9
How much do ferrets cost?   10

Chapter 3: Living With Ferrets   12
Preparing to adopt a ferret and
   understanding the nature of ferrets   12
Dangerous areas in the average household   12
Are ferrets good pets for children?   13
Do ferrets get along with other pets?   14
Is there something wrong with my ferret?   14
Do ferrets bite?   16

Chapter 4: Acquiring a ferret   17
Where can I get a ferret?   17
Source #1. Pet shops   17
SOURCE #2. Small breeders   18
SOURCE #3. Ferret shelters   18
Selecting a particular ferret   19

Chapter 5: Bringing Your Ferret Home   20
Ferret-proofing a house   20
Care for pet shop ferrets   20
Housing   21

Chapter 6: Feeding Your Ferret   23
What to feed your ferret   23
How you should feed your ferret   23
Snacks   24

Chapter 7: Socializing Your Ferret   25
Safe toys for ferrets   25
Training your ferret   25
Litter training   26

Chapter 8: Grooming   27
Controlling loose hair   27
Controlling ferret odor   27
Bathing a ferret   27
Ear care   28
Scruffing   28
Nail trimming   29
Restraint for nail trimming   29

Chapter 9: Health Care and Program   30
Schedule of veterinary care for baby ferrets   30
Veterinary care for adult ferrets   30
What about spaying or neutering?   31
What difference does descenting make?   32
Teeth and teething   32
My ferret is going bald!   33
Itchy ferrets   34
First aid for ferrets   34
What to keep in your ferret's medicine cabinet   36

Chapter 10: Going Places and Doing Things   37
Traveling   37
Boarding   38
Ferret shows   39

Chapter 11: Reproduction And Growth of Ferrets   40
Reproduction   41
Kits from birth to sexual maturity   41
Congenital problems and genetic defects   41

Chapter 12: Ferret Nutrition   43
Importance of a good diet   43
What you can learn from the label on a bag of food   43
Special feeding requirements   44

Chapter 13: Parasites   47
Intestinal parasites   47
Heartworm disease   47
External parasites   48

Chapter 14: Common Illnesses   50
Respiratory infections   50
Diarrhea   50
Vomiting   53

Chapter 15: Two Viral Diseases That Kill Ferrets   54
Canine distemper   54
Rabies   54

Chapter 16: Three Common Types of Cancer in Ferrets   56
Lymphosarcoma   56
Adrenal gland cancer   56
Insulinomas   57

Chapter 17:
When It's Time To Say Good-Bye   58

Glossary   59

Appendix A - Medications Commonly Used In Ferrets   62

Appendix B - Areas Where Pet Ferrets Are Illegal   63

Appendix C - Resources For Ferret Owners   63

INTRODUCING THE DOMESTIC FERRET

WHAT IS A FERRET?

A ferret is a small mammal, usually weighing less than 5 pounds. Females (jills) are much smaller than males (hobs), averaging 1.5 to 2 pounds at maturity. The scientific name for the domestic ferret is *Mustela putorius furo*. Ferrets are not rodents and are not even related to rodents. They are carnivorous animals (meat eaters) in the same biologic grouping as cats and dogs. Neutered males are called gibs and spayed jills are sprites. Babies are called kits.

Sable jill

WHO OWNS FERRETS?

Ferrets have become the third most popular house pet in the USA, and their owners now represent a large cross-section of America. Most pet ferret owners are upper middle class or professional people who work all day. Frequently they are single women or childless couples over 30 years of age. Generally ferrets are pets of adults, not children, although children in the family usually like and play with the ferrets too.

WHERE DO FERRETS COME FROM - ARE THERE ANY WILD ONES?

Domestic ferrets are related to mink and weasels and to the black-footed ferret, a wild, weasel-like animal native to North America. *Mustela putorius furo*, the domestic ferret, has been domesticated for thousands of years, as long as the cat and dog. There are no wild ones anywhere. These animals are called mustelids because their anal glands secrete a strong smelling musk. The first domesticated ferrets probably originated from captive breeding of wild polecats, which still exist in Europe and Asia. There are pictures in Egyptian tombs of ferret-like creatures on leashes. After thousands of generations of domestication, ferrets have no inherent fear of man, and cannot survive without human aid. They are smaller than polecats and although the two species can be cross-bred and produce hybrid babies, they are genetically different. Ferrets are much smaller and more agile than cats

Siamese jill with fluffy winter coat

and can follow rodents into smaller holes. This was probably the reason people thought of catching polecats, breeding them and keeping the friendliest ones in their homes and barns. About three hundred years ago, the first ferrets worked their way to North America from Europe, controlling rodents on the ships of the early colonists. There are still a few ferrets on rat patrol in dairy barns and ships in Canada and the US. Although hunting with ferrets is illegal in America now, they have been used to hunt burrowing animals such as rabbits and groundhogs. The ferret does not usually kill the prey: it chases it out of the burrow where it is captured or killed by some human means. Occasionally ferrets pull electric or telephone wires through long ducts too small for more conventional methods to be efficient.

Large Siamese hob with winter coat

COAT COLORS

Black-eyed white and Albino kits

There are two basic colors of ferrets, sable and albino. Albino ferrets are unpigmented, having pure white fur and pink eyes.

All kits have white hair at birth, but the albinos remain white and colored ferrets turn grey during their first week of life. They do not have a distinctive coat until they are about four weeks old. Even then, their adult color cannot accurately be predicted.

Sable ferrets are similar to wild polecats in color. They have black legs and tails, with a mixture of white or yellow underfur and dark brown or black guard hair on their bodies. The dark mask around their eyes gives them a distinctive appearance. Babies develop their masks when they are about two weeks old, but they have a band of dark hair between their eyes until they are mature: this is one way to distinguish a young ferret from an adult. All colored ferrets change color when they molt. Some will have a distinctly different summer color, and return to the original color with the fall molt. Siamese is just a lighter color phase of sable. Siamese ferrets have brown hair where sables have black. People who show ferrets have named different shades of sable and Siamese, for instance butterscotch is a very pale shade of Siamese, cinnamon is a very red Siamese, and chocolate is rich dark brown. A black sable has almost no light color in its coat, and from a distance appears solid black.

This 3-year-old sterling silver jill had much more dark hair when she was younger. Eventually she will look pure white.

There are many mutations of color in ferrets producing a wide range of shades and patterns. Silver ferrets have no distinct division in color between their bodies and feet; they are silver all over. When young, these ferrets might look sable or Siamese, but they often have small spots of white on their hind legs, and there will be some white through their coats if you look hard. Silver mitts are grey ferrets with white paws. Silvers have variable amounts of white mixed with dark hair, but all of them fade with time. Silver mitts may start out as sable or Siamese ferrets with white feet, and get more white in their coats with every molt. Some silvers appear white at birth but have a few dark hairs down the middle of their backs or on their heads, which vanish with a few molts. Eventually, silver ferrets become almost pure white. Dark-eyed ferrets that are born pure white are known as black-eyed whites to distinguish them from albinos.

Some ferrets are solid sable or Siamese, but have white streaks on their heads or have almost white heads, lacking masks entirely or having just a ring of color around each eye. At ferret shows these are called pandas. Pandas may have white mitts, and many have white around their necks or on their chests or bellies.

Occasionally odd-colored ferrets are born, with rings of white on their tails, with one or more white toes on each foot, or with patches of color on a white body.

This jill is a mitt: her body color is Siamese and all 4 paws are white

A panda often has no mask at all. This Siamese panda has only "spectacles" around her eyes.

HOW LONG DO FERRETS LIVE?

The average ferret that is fed a good diet and receives regular veterinary care lives to be 6 or 7 years old. Some live to be 8 or 9 and occasionally even older. Ferrets that are allowed to go outside are at much greater risk of injury and disease than inside pets.

Although their panda markings are evident and they appear to be Siamese, the exact adult color of these 4 week old kits is impossible to predict. Notice the fluffy baby "mane" on the backs of their necks.

HOW MUCH CARE DOES A FERRET NEED?

A ferret requires very little special care to be comfortable. It must have food and fresh water constantly available. It prefers a snug nest to sleep in. It needs a litter box, which should be cleaned at least once daily, or some other toilet arrangement that requires cleaning, such as papers on the floor. Caged ferrets need to be allowed out to play for an hour or two every day in a room that has been ferret-proofed. Young, healthy ferrets can be left alone for a weekend with a dependable water source and enough food to last the time they are unobserved, although it is safer to have someone check on them once daily.

chapter 2

BENEFITS AND COSTS OF FERRET OWNERSHIP

FERRETS MAKE GOOD PETS

Ferrets require neither human nor ferret company for security or amusement most of the time. They are not nocturnal, but go to sleep when nothing exciting is happening, and wake up whenever a human comes to entertain or be entertained by them. They do not become neurotic as some other house pets do when left alone for long periods of time. Cats or dogs may suffer from self-inflicted injuries by licking constantly at a paw or leg when bored: ferrets never do this. They can be left with an adequate supply of food and water and will be quite happy to spend their days alone. Thus they are excellent pets for people who go to work early in the morning and don't get home until evening. They require little out-of-cage exercise and no out-of-doors exercise, and are much safer when kept inside.

Young kits need to sleep a lot. Give your new kit a chance to rest undisturbed after a long play session.

Because they can be caged, ferrets can be prevented from damaging the house while their owners are away. Apartment landlords often accept a ferret as a cage-dweller like a hamster or guinea pig even if it really spends most of its time free in the house when the owner is at home.

Ferrets are quiet. They make very few sounds after they are 6 or 8 weeks old. Neighbors in an apartment nearby would not hear any vocalization, although the ferrets might rattle the door of their cage when they hear their owner returning home.

A single pet ferret may be very happy with only human company, and becomes devoted to the major person in its life. However, most ferrets are compatible, multiple housing is feasible, and groups of ferrets are great fun to watch. They usually prefer to sleep together and readily share their food. Ferret-watching becomes a regular and favorite pastime for the owners. Ferrets do not require as much human attention when they are allowed to play together and amuse each other.

Ferrets can be litter or paper trained, with some patience. They are clean animals to have in a house or apartment. Although they are not as reliable as cats, they will usually use a litter box in their cage. When free in the house, ferrets select a few corners as toilet areas, and will train you to put litter boxes or paper in those spots.

WHAT DO PEOPLE LIKE ABOUT FERRETS?

Ferrets are very playful animals that act silly and express their love of life in a way that many of us find totally enchanting. They explode out of their cages at play time, leaping and twisting and scampering, with an obvious joy that makes people observing them feel good. They may also be very affectionate, especially as they grow older, and enjoy being picked up and cuddled. Whatever they see you doing, they want to do it with you. They think everything in the house is put there for their amusement. They steal socks and keys and hide them in inaccessible places. They never pass a wastebasket without overturning it. They climb inside chairs or couches at each opportunity. They can't resist nibbling bare toes. They always do a dance of joy when let out to play, or when approached by their person of significance. They like to go to sleep in tiny corners or unexpected places. Many ferrets like to take a nap in a bureau drawer full of clothes or the bottom of a basket full of laundry, leaving a few whiskers or a limp paw visible to charm their owners. Just his way of moving, like a large furry inchworm, endears a ferret to his owner. Pets learn what to expect from their owners,

Ferrets are curious and persistent. They can't resist overturning an upright container like a wastebasket.

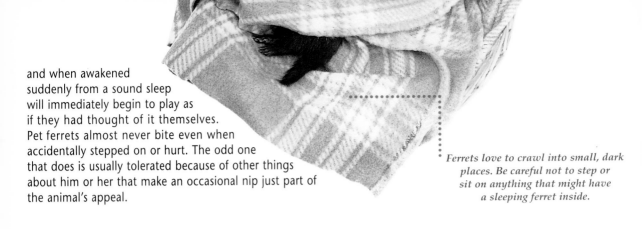

and when awakened
suddenly from a sound sleep
will immediately begin to play as
if they had thought of it themselves.
Pet ferrets almost never bite even when
accidentally stepped on or hurt. The odd one
that does is usually tolerated because of other things
about him or her that make an occasional nip just part of
the animal's appeal.

Ferrets love to crawl into small, dark places. Be careful not to step or sit on anything that might have a sleeping ferret inside.

HOW MUCH DO FERRETS COST?

The smallest expense that will be incurred by the owner of a ferret is the purchase price, whether it is acquired from a pet shop or private breeder as a baby, or as an adult from a shelter. Responsible pet ownership does not depend on the monetary value of the animal measured by the purchase price. It is fulfillment of an unwritten contract you enter when you decide to own a living creature that will depend entirely on you for its well-being. This is true of any pet, whether it is a mongrel acquired free from a neighbor or a purebred show animal bought at great price from a prominent breeder. Your responsibility includes providing adequate housing, food, exercise, and veterinary care for the pet, and making sure it is physically protected from infectious diseases and harmful substances, activities, people, or other animals. It is also your legal responsibility to prevent your animal from harming other people or their property, by confining the pet as necessary.

Feeding ferrets is not a large expense but they require good quality food for health, and this should not be an area to save money. Generic cat foods cause several kinds of health problems, and ferrets will die in a short time if fed only dog food. The best ferret foods will be available in pet shops or from ferret clubs.

Pet ferrets need to be spayed or neutered. Descenting is an option that many people choose. The cost of these surgical procedures varies from place to place. Most pet shops sell kits that have already been spayed or neutered and descented.

Ferret toys and elaborate cages are not really necessary for the ferret's comfort. If he is allowed out to play for several hours every day, the ferret can tolerate a very small cage, as he will only eat, sleep and use a litterbox in it. A guinea pig cage will suffice if the pet gets adequate exercise in a larger area. Fancy sleeping tubes and hammocks are not required, but provide much comfort to the ferret and satisfaction to the owner. Left to choose for themselves, ferrets will select very small simple nests such as a winter hat or an empty paper bag. Many ferrets prefer an old sweatshirt to a relatively expensive sleeping tube. If you keep your pets in a prominent place in your living area, it is desirable to have professionally built ferret cages and equipment.

Ferrets do not suffer from many serious diseases early in life, but canine distemper is deadly. Ferrets require yearly vaccination: unvaccinated ferrets usually die if infected with canine distemper virus.

Older ferrets become susceptible to several types of cancer that may be treatable by surgical and/or medical means, although these can be expensive. The life span of the ferret is only 6 or 7 years, but people become devoted to their pet in a short time and are usually willing to provide whatever care is necessary, whatever the cost may be. Someone who owns several ferrets may have sizable veterinary bills as the animals age.

These are the only vaccines approved for use in ferrets.

Some states and municipal areas require licenses for ferrets kept as pets. Some states forbid the keeping of ferrets as pets and there are stiff penalties for defying the law. The ferret often pays the stiffest penalty: it may be seized and killed by the authorities.

Although there is an effective rabies vaccine for ferrets, public health departments do not recognize the ferret as a domestic animal like a cat. In many municipalities, if a ferret bites or scratches someone who makes a complaint or seeks medical attention, the animal is killed and tested for rabies. Ferret owners have fought the seizure of their pet in court and won, but lawyers' fees and other legal costs have taken their life savings and everything they owned. This is an avoidable expense if you prevent your ferret from contacting strangers.

FOR MORE INFORMATION ON . . .

feeding, see chapters 6 and 12

spaying and neutering, see chapter 9

rabies and distemper, see chapters 9 and 15

cancer, see chapter 16

areas where ferrets are illegal, see Appendix B

chapter 3

LIVING WITH FERRETS

PREPARING TO ADOPT A FERRET AND UNDERSTANDING THE NATURE OF THE FERRET

Hopefully you will be reading this before you have selected a ferret and taken it home. It is not safe for either the animal or the dwelling to turn a ferret loose in the average home without some ferret-proofing. This list of ferret characteristics is universally true. Take the advice seriously to protect your pet and your home.

Ferrets rarely chew house plants (which may be poisonous), but love to dig the soil out of the pot.

Ferrets are curious: they will inspect small spaces that you might not ordinarily be aware of and crawl into them. They can get under kitchen cabinets and appliances and get stuck, or chew electrical wires and electrocute themselves.

Ferrets are burrowing animals: they like to find snug dark areas to sleep in. They may sleep very soundly and don't wake up even when you call long and loud.

Ferrets are very persistent: when they find something they want to do, it is nearly impossible to discourage them from continuing to do it, even if it is dangerous. The only way to stop them is to remove access to the area of interest.

Ferrets are agile: they can fit their bodies through any space where their heads will go. They can bend and twist to get through very small spaces and won't come out until they are ready.

Ferrets are almost fearless: until they learn about heights, they will walk off the edges of tables and furniture without hesitation. If they have no reason to fear other animals, they will walk right up to a dog or cat that may immediately grab and kill them. They may fall into water and although they can swim, they will drown if there is no way out of the enclosure. Some ferrets will try to jump across distances that they estimate poorly and can fall onto hard surfaces. Some ferrets will climb to the top of a piece of furniture but don't know how to get down. It has been claimed that ferrets are poor climbers, but in fact it's only coming down that they find awkward.

DANGEROUS AREAS IN THE AVERAGE HOUSEHOLD THAT COULD SERIOUSLY HURT OR KILL A FERRET INCLUDE, BUT ARE NOT LIMITED TO:

A belled collar helps to locate a moving ferret, but can cause a fatal accident if he gets caught inside a confined space.

Furniture: ferrets like to climb inside chairs and couches and tear out the stuffing. They also get behind heavy furniture to take a nap and will not wake up or come out even when you call them. Many ferrets have been smothered under chair cushions or killed by rocking chairs or recliners when someone unaware of the ferret's presence sits down or changes the position of the chair, catching the ferret in the mechanism.

Appliances: ferrets can get into areas of washers, driers, stoves and fridges that expose the animal to moving parts or electrical wires, or they may get stuck on projections and be unable to get back out. This is particularly dangerous for ferrets that wear collars.

Open driers: ferrets like to get into a drier full of clothes and will be trapped there if it is turned on. The heat will kill them in minutes. They also like to crawl into clothes baskets and may be put into the machine with the wash by someone unaware of their presence.

Windows: they can crawl up on sills and fall out if the window is left open, or if it has a sliding screen that ferret paws can move aside.

Air ducts: if the ferret can get access to a duct he will travel wherever it goes and may not know how to get out. Eventually he will become dehydrated and die if not found. If you live in an apartment building, he may come out in the home of a stranger who will kill him, or take him to a shelter or pound instead of looking for the owner within the building. Ferrets are mistaken for rats or squirrels by some people and chased outside or beaten to death with brooms or other handy weapons. Extermination chemicals intended for other animals will kill ferrets.

Open doors: ferrets that get outside move quickly and are rarely able to find their way home. They carelessly cross streets and get run over by vehicles. They are often killed by dogs or cats, or by people who don't like them or don't recognize them as pets. They may be picked up by municipal pounds and destroyed without a waiting period, as this is the policy in many cities. They are very unlikely to survive in a hot climate even if they can find food. There is rarely a source of food available in the city. They may kill domestic fowl if they find them and then are likely to be killed by the owner of the birds.

NEVER LET YOUR FERRET RUN LOOSE OUTSIDE ON PURPOSE AND DO EVERYTHING NECESSARY TO PREVENT ACCIDENTAL ESCAPES.

ARE FERRETS GOOD PETS FOR CHILDREN?

Ferrets do not like to be restrained and prefer to do exactly as they please most of the time. The younger the ferret, the less likely it is to be cuddly. The normal behavior for just-weaned kits is to wrestle and chew on each other most of their waking moments. They will try to do this with people, too, and may bite hard enough to cause pain without intending to hurt you. Children are more likely than adults to panic and yank their hands back, causing more serious bites that break the skin. Kits can be taught not to bite but it takes time, as it does for puppies and kittens. This is one reason ferrets are not ideal pets for children too young or too active to learn to play gently with a ferret and not to encourage it to rough-house as it does with its littermates.

Older ferrets will tolerate much indignity and may be long-suffering in the hands of children they learn to trust. A child who suddenly and roughly tries to pick up or hold onto a ferret that doesn't want to be restrained may get bitten. This is most likely with kits up to 9 or 10 months of age, when they are at their most active and never want to be still. Many older pets are surprisingly tolerant of unusually rough handling by strangers.

Children are rarely responsible enough to make sure the ferret can't get out of the safety of his play area, and don't realize how easily a small animal may be fatally injured by being crushed in a recliner or door. Ferrets are not good pets for children who do not have responsible and knowledgeable adult supervision.

This child knows how to handle her ferret and they are comfortable with each other. Toddlers or babies can frighten ferrets and may be severely bitten.

NEVER LEAVE A YOUNG CHILD UNATTENDED WITH A FERRET.

DO FERRETS GET ALONG WITH OTHER PETS?

Ferrets and cats are carnivores and predators. Don't assume that they will cohabit with natural prey such as rodents, rabbits and birds. To avoid unpleasant accidents, these species should never be left with an unattended ferret or cat.

It is also wise never to expose a ferret to a terrier or other type of hunting dog likely to kill what it sees as small vermin. Some dogs will tolerate a ferret while the owner is present but will attack it when the two pets are alone, especially if the ferret approaches the dog's food or favorite toy. This is natural behavior for many breeds of dogs. Dogs within a breed vary widely and must be evaluated individually. No animal can be expected to have a conscience or be concerned about human values. Owners must take these responsibilities for their pets.

Ferrets have been introduced to and cohabited safely and happily with many kinds of pets, most commonly cats and dogs. Ferrets like to tease other animals by nipping at their feet or tails, or running underneath them and grabbing them by the neck or belly and hanging on. These are ferret games that initially alarm other pets. The first few times ferrets are exposed to other family pets there should be close supervision. The dog or cat can be allowed to observe the ferret safely shut in its cage, where the animals can see and smell each other but not touch. Well-trained dogs can be taught to leave the ferret alone no matter what it does, but undisciplined dogs may have to be kept away when the ferret leaves its cage. Cats are rarely able to hurt an adult ferret but

Dogs and cats can cohabit safely with ferrets, but should be carefully supervised until they are well acquainted.

can easily kill a kit. Ferrets can move very quickly and slip through tiny openings that other animals cannot negotiate. Cats and ferrets living under one roof usually come to a mutually satisfactory arrangement. They learn to play together and invent games that are as entertaining for those observing as they are for the participants.

If the housing area does not overcrowd them there is no limit to the number of ferrets you can house together. Some individuals may not be as sociable as others and, although it's a rare event, serious personality clashes may arise. Incompatible ferrets that have wrestling and chattering matches don't usually hurt each other but may have to be housed and allowed out for exercise separately to avoid owner anxiety. Ferret skin is very tough and resists penetration of teeth and claws. Even after what seems like a pitched battle between two rival ferrets, there is seldom a mark on either combatant.

When new ferrets are added to an established group, you can expect a few challenges to the newcomer. Most senior ferrets accept young ones very well, and may be rejuvenated by the enthusiasm of a youthful companion. Older ferrets have much less stamina than a young kit or juvenile, and usually try to hide after a short time of very active play. Young ferrets don't wear out easily and the older one may have to be protected by returning him to his cage when he has had enough exercise.

IS THERE SOMETHING WRONG WITH MY FERRET?

This is not a discussion of ferret diseases. Ferrets do things sometimes that make new owners think that their pet has a serious problem.

Ferrets of all ages like to sleep in a pile.

• Sometimes ferrets sleep so soundly that they seem to be dead. You can pick them up, shake them, pinch their toes, or thump them on the chest, and they hang from your hand as limp as rags, with their eyes closed. About the time you've run to the car on the way to the nearest emergency veterinary clinic, the ferret sleepily opens its eyes and looks innocently around, wondering what's going on. Some ferrets do this quite commonly and their owners get used to it. Others just do it occasionally, and each time, their person of significance panics because they are afraid their pet is in a coma or has died.

• Often when you wake your ferret up and take it out of its cage, it trembles. People sometimes interpret this as fear, or shivering because the room is too cold. Adult ferrets tremble with excitement, anticipation, and probably other pleasurable ferret emotions that we can't adequately describe in words. They rarely shiver with cold, and fear is expressed differently. Don't turn up the heat, just be happy that your ferret is glad to see you.

• Ferrets sleep in very strange positions, making it seem that they have a physical problem preventing them from lying down normally. They may sleep draped face down across the sharp edge of a box or other container, with their heads and front legs on the floor. Sometimes they lie on their stomachs, bent backwards at a 90° angle up the side of a sleeping container or box. This looks awkward to us, but it is apparently comfortable for ferrets, as many of them sleep that way when they have other choices of location and position.

• Ferrets like to sleep together for comfort, and in cold weather, for warmth. When given several containers to sleep in, a group of ferrets will usually all get into one. This doesn't mean that there's anything wrong with the other beds. Whoever gets in first ends up on the bottom, and never suffocates although it appears to be a risk.

• When first released from their cages to play, many ferrets burst out of the door, run and leap and twist in the air, and carelessly collide with solid objects. They might run over to your feet, nip at your shoe, and go on another race around the room, sometimes making soft chuckling noises as they do. They don't try to avoid running into things, and show no signs of pain even when they hit solid objects with a thump. New owners have feared that these ferrets are having convulsions, have rabies, or have gone blind. However, it is normal ferret behavior, expressing exuberance at being let out to play, and is a good indicator that the ferret is feeling well. Ferrets have a very high threshold of pain and truly do not appear to notice bumps that would make most other animals stop and lick the spot that was hurt.

• After using the litter box, most ferrets drag their hindquarters along the floor, the way dogs do when they have impacted anal glands. Owners sometimes take the ferret to a veterinarian thinking it has a problem with its descenting surgery, or that it is itchy, or constipated, or is losing control of its hind legs. None of these is the answer. Your ferret is just using your rug for toilet paper, a good reason for locating the litter box on a floor that can easily be washed.

DO FERRETS BITE?

Play-biting of kits: Most baby animals chew and mouth things and ferrets are no exception. Kits play by wrestling and gripping each other's necks with their teeth. Until they learn otherwise, they expect to do this with people too. Babies also may bite hard if they are very hungry, because they haven't learned what is food.

Fear reaction: Young ferrets may be frightened by sudden movement from above, especially accompanied by a loud noise. This is probably a reflex inherited from their wild ancestors, the weasels and polecats, who were preyed on mainly by large birds. A fear reaction in a young ferret is dramatic. He will hunch his back, open his mouth and hiss, fluff out the hair on his tail, and sometimes screech, a sound that alarms other ferrets in the area. If he is not descented, he may release the strong smelling substance in his anal sacs. This whole series of events is a defense reaction designed to scare off the attacker. If you grab at a ferret during this reaction he may bite you very hard, because he thinks he is in real danger. Older ferrets rarely show this reaction unless truly attacked by another animal, and some become so trusting they don't even do it then. Talk quietly to a kit that shows a fear reaction, and don't try to pick him up unless it is necessary to save him from falling or escaping outside. In a few minutes he will realize it's a false alarm and go back to his normal self.

Juvenile play: Ferrets have sharp teeth and can hurt you if they bite and hang on. Juvenile males occasionally try to do this to people, as they do with each other. Human skin is not nearly as thick as ferret hide, and we have no protective hair covering, so that kind of treatment causes real pain. The harder you try to pull the ferret loose, the tighter he will hold on, enjoying the challenge of the game. You can't pry the ferret's teeth apart because he has very strong jaws and is very determined. Sometimes if you press the ferret's lips against his molar teeth he will release his grip long enough to free yourself. There are several other tricks to make a biting ferret let go.

You can discourage some ferrets that haven't tried this game before by snapping them hard on the end of the nose. Smacking them anywhere on the body will usually cause them to hang on tighter. Being shaken vigorously often discourages them. Those that won't let go with a shake or a nose snap will usually turn loose if you put them under running water, head first. Occasionally a really determined one thinks this is just part of the game and grimly hangs on anyway. The last resort is to put something either very bitter or very sweet in the ferret's mouth with the blunt end of a pencil or pen. Sometimes the pencil itself tastes interesting and the ferret will let go of your arm or hand to try something new. It is better not to use a sweet treat if you can avoid it, as rewarding the ferret for biting is not your goal. It will work as a diversion if there is no handy alternative.

Ferrets that are adopted as kits rarely develop this kind of biting habit because you can discourage the mouthing of human hands before it becomes a problem. A male adopted when half grown, especially at 12 to 16 weeks of age, is more likely to bite because he has been playing rough games with his ferret companions who don't object very much. It is less common for jills and neutered males to behave this way, but ferrets are individuals and no generalizations can be made.

Some jills with babies will attack people who reach into the nest to pick up their kits, a justifiable defense on their part. They, too, hang on, intending to hurt you as much as possible. The best way to avoid this kind of bite is not to disturb a jill with newborn kits.

Young ferrets naturally wrestle and chew on each other at every opportunity but should be discouraged from mouthing human fingers. Rough play encourages ferrets to bite.

chapter 4

ACQUIRING A FERRET

WHERE CAN I GET A FERRET?
There are three main sources of ferrets.

SOURCE #1 PET SHOPS Many pet shops sell baby ferrets that come from professional breeders, already spayed or neutered and descented. They come in a great variety of coat colors and usually have been bred for good temperament.

Advantages of buying a ferret at a pet shop:
- The kit is young and you can experience the full range of ferret life with it, from cuddly baby to active and often obnoxious juvenile to the distinctive personality that comes with maturation.
- The kit is already spayed or neutered and descented, sparing you the responsibility and expense of having this done later.
- You usually have a choice of sex and colors, and if the current selection isn't quite what you want, there will be more the next time the shop gets ferrets in.

These 7-week-old kits (2 Siamese and a Silver) have just arrived at a pet shop, spayed or neutered and descented, ready for adoption.

- If a problem develops in the first few weeks of owning the ferret, pet shops and their suppliers will replace the animal for you: small breeders often do not have anything to replace it with.
- Many large chains of pet shops have very knowledgeable personnel who can give good advice on nutrition, housing, and health, and have access to more expert help when necessary.
- Pet shops usually keep a range of ferret food, toys and other equipment that you can see in use and purchase at the same time as the kit.

Disadvantages of buying from a pet shop:
- You have no idea what the kit's parents were like.
- Some pet shop employees do not take the time or have the knowledge to explain how to care for a ferret or what to expect from it. It depends very much on the specific pet shop what the quality of care and knowledge will be.
- Some people believe that early spaying and neutering of kits makes them more susceptible to adrenal gland tumors later. This may be so, but both unspayed and unneutered ferrets and those altered when more mature also get adrenal gland tumors. No research has been done to decide if there is a connection between adrenal tumors and the early spaying and neutering of ferrets.

SOURCE #2 SMALL BREEDERS Smaller breeders, who keep only a few jills, raise one or two litters a year from each. Some of these people take their ferrets to shows and specialize in a particular coat color or pattern. They usually sell kits a little older than those available in pet shops, and they are not spayed, neutered or descented when you buy them. Sometimes you can buy a jill that has been retired from breeding, if you want to start with a more experienced ferret.

Advantages of buying from a small breeder:
- You can see the parents of the ferret you are getting. There is no guarantee that the kits will be exactly like their parents but personalities tend to be similar, especially those of the jill and her kits.
- Most people who raise ferrets know quite a bit about them, and are eager to supply the new owner with information.
- People who raise only a few litters are usually interested in what becomes of the kits they sell.

Disadvantages of buying from small breeders:
- Ferrets naturally breed only in the spring and early summer. Most small breeders have their ferrets in their home where it is not so easy to control lighting for the animals. Larger ferret producers keep their breeding colony under artificial lighting, which makes it possible to raise kits year-round. Kits are usually available from small breeders only in the natural breeding season.

Small breeders may raise only 1 or 2 litters a year, usually of a narrow color range, but you probably can see the mother, the littermates, and sometimes other siblings before selecting your pet.

- Any particular breeder has only a few varieties of colors or patterns to choose from.
- Some small breeders have pet theories (the proverbial "old wives' tales") that are not based on facts, or are partial truths limited by the extent of their experience. New ferret owners who believe everything one person tells them without looking for other sources of information may be misled, and the disadvantage may be to their ferret.

SOURCE #3 FERRET SHELTERS Ferret shelters rescue and offer for adoption ferrets that have been lost, abandoned, or for some reason given up by the original owner.

Advantages of adopting a ferret from a shelter:
- It is usually an adult already litter trained and with its personality well defined.
- It is a ferret in need that might otherwise be destroyed. Some are brought in from areas where ferrets are illegal after the owner was given the option of sending the ferret out of state instead of surrendering it and having it destroyed.
- Animals are usually neutered or spayed and properly vaccinated before leaving the shelter.
- First time owners can be "trained" by adopting one of these experienced ferrets, and usually then go out and buy some more ferrets to liven up their home and light up their lives.
- The fee for adopting these ferrets is usually very low, barely enough to cover the cost of looking after a normal ferret. Shelters depend on donations of food, litter, toys, and money to keep going. It is not a profitable enterprise.
- These shelters are run by ferret enthusiasts who often sacrifice their own time and money to make sure each ferret gets a fair trial and if possible a good home. They often keep the sick or "bad" ferrets for long periods of time to rehabilitate them, to make sure they can be adopted out. They are willing to counsel new owners and may refuse to allow certain ferrets to go to a particular owner because their experience tells them it would not be a good relationship. They are usually willing to take back ferrets that don't work out in the new home.

Disadvantages of adopting a ferret from a shelter:

- Some of these animals have behavior problems that the first owner could not tolerate and was unable to deal with. Some have health problems that the owner did not want to spend money on. Many are older ferrets with a short life expectancy.

SELECTING A PARTICULAR FERRET

If you have never owned or spent much time with a ferret, there are some things you need to know before adopting one. Some practical aspects of housing and cohabitation with other pets have already been dealt with. There are other considerations.

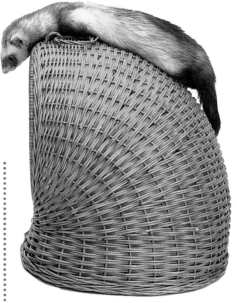

Do you have any animal experience?

If you have little experience handling animals, a baby ferret may not be a good choice. They are cute and cuddly in the pet shop, but in a few weeks they will be juveniles. These perpetual motion machines are reluctant to sit still even for a moment, and appear determined to destroy your house and everything in it. They are careless of their own safety and that of your belongings. This can be a bewildering metamorphosis for first-time ferret owners, and it results in some of these young ferrets being abandoned or taken to shelters. Ferrets do grow out of this stage, females often sooner than males, but it may take a year. The more ferrets you have, the

This 4-year-old Siamese jill lost a hind leg in an accident when she was very young. A physical handicap rarely prevents a ferret from living a normal, active life.

less you will notice manic behavior in a young one, because the ferrets use their energy playing wild games with each other. If you're not used to living with animals, and don't think you can get through this stage, don't adopt a baby until you've had more experience. Get a healthy mature ferret from a shelter or a retired breeder from a private ferretry.

Do you have a lot of time, love and money to devote to your pet?

People who like to back losers are happiest with an older ferret with a health problem that requires constant attention. Would you like to give tender loving care to an animal that will return your affection and never complain, even when it must have treatments that make it temporarily more uncomfortable? Can you deal with losing it despite your efforts? Then adopt a chronically ill ferret from a shelter. It will provide a home for an animal that deserves one as well as giving you a chance to do what you're best at.

Are you a true animal lover?

True animal lovers tolerate anything a juvenile ferret can dish out, and grow to love it because of its exuberant behavior. These people usually have multiple ferrets and enjoy the antics of the young ones. Pet shop ferrets make wonderful pets for these homes. You can watch them grow into juveniles, then into adults, and learn more about ferrets every day. This type of person is also good at taking on ferrets with behavior problems.

Do you like to get involved with others who share your interests?

Ferret shows are great fun for ferret enthusiasts, but they do put the animals at risk from infectious diseases. Some people thrive on competition and enjoy getting their pets out where they can be seen. Small breeders usually start this way, and they are the ones who might be most able to supply you with "show ferrets." There are classes for neutered pet shop animals as well, but if you're really interested in getting into the ferret business, it might be best to follow the shows and buy from a breeder.

FOR MORE INFORMATION ON . . .

ferret shelters, see Appendix C

chapter 5

BRINGING YOUR FERRET HOME

FERRET-PROOFING A HOUSE

A pet ferret should be confined to a cage when there is no human supervision, or to a thoroughly ferret-proofed room from which there is no escape.

- Check for loose air duct covers and secure as necessary.
- Close off the areas under kitchen counters, which usually have an inch or two clearance above the floor. This is a favorite place for ferrets to go to sleep. If there is no human access to it, the ferret cannot be recovered from these areas without dismantling the whole counter.
- Make sure all windows are kept closed or securely screened. Remember a small ferret can squeeze through a hole only a bit over an inch in diameter.
- Cover the backs of appliances with screening if the ferret will have access to rooms where appliances are kept.
- Use child-proof fasteners on all cupboard doors where there are dangerous chemicals, or where there are spaces around plumbing that a ferret could squeeze through.

Be sure your cupboard doors are fastened securely or contain no ferret hazards such as toxic cleaning products or small holes around pipes.

- Put hooks on sliding doors to rooms where the ferret should not go: most ferrets quickly learn how to move sliding doors.
- Prevent access to balconies where there is anything less than a solid smooth barrier to prevent ferrets from falling. This will include stairwells.
- Keep toilet lids down, or keep ferrets out of the bathroom.
- Have no exposed electric cords on the floor of a room where the ferrets play by themselves. Ferrets like to drag things around and may chew and tug on a cord hard and long enough to be electrocuted.

CARE FOR PET SHOP FERRETS

Baby ferrets arrive at pet shops when they are only 7 weeks old. They generally have travelled by both plane and truck to get there. Depending on the season, they may have been very hot or too cold for hours at a time. They may have had surgery a week before, and have been moved into different groups of other ferrets a few times by the day of their arrival. At the pet shop, they are exposed to other species of animals, usually dogs and cats and often reptiles and birds as well. Their cage is unfamiliar and they may be given bedding and food different from what they are used to. The temperature in the pet shop may be too warm and dry for them. There are new sounds and smells and

many people looking at them and sometimes handling them when they just want to sleep or eat. Their whole routine is changed.

Fortunately ferrets have a very philosophical outlook. They enjoy new experiences if they have food and a comfortable place to sleep. However, all the changes they experience are stressful. Stress increases susceptibility to respiratory infections and parasites at a time when they are exposed to new infections and parasites from some people or animals they meet.

Most of the time, pet shop ferrets remain healthy. To minimize stress, allow your new ferret time to adjust to his new home. Don't let everyone in the neighborhood come in and handle him. Keep him in a cool, not a very warm area, and make sure he has a cozy nest to sleep in. Cover the cage floor with newspaper, not shavings which may cause sneezing and interfere with litter training.

Before you bring your kit home:

Have a cage ready for him, that should contain:
1) a litter box with a very low entrance.
2) a water bottle and a clip-on dish of water.
3) a food container (crock or clip-on), with the food he's accustomed to.
4) a sleeping tube or other nest.

Sometimes kits get colds at the pet shop or while travelling through airports on their way there. The kit may be normal for a day or two after you take him home, then starts sneezing. He will get better much sooner if he has a cool, quiet spot to live in. If your new ferret starts to sneeze and has a runny nose a few days after bringing him home, keep his nose clean so that he can breathe, make sure he can eat, and moisten his food with warm water to make it more palatable. If he seems very sick or has a persistent runny nose with a yellow or white discharge, make an appointment to have a veterinarian examine him. Most ferrets with colds, like most people, feel much better after 3 or 4 days. Sometimes they need antibiotics to help clear up the infection.

This cage is ready for its new occupant. The small cat litter pan has been cut down on one side to allow easy access by a small ferret. The water dish is raised off the floor and is firmly clipped to the cage, and there is a water bottle also available. A sleeping tube and nest box, both fastened to the cage wire, are provided.

A pet shop kit has probably had a temporary distemper vaccination before leaving the breeding farm, but this is not going to protect him after he is 9 weeks old. He must receive at least two, and preferably three distemper vaccinations, to protect him against this deadly disease. Find out how old the kit is before leaving the shop, so you will know when to schedule his vaccinations. Until he has had two vaccinations, protect him from exposure to distemper virus by not allowing him outside, even on a leash. Minimize contact with dogs, or with strangers who can carry the virus to him on their hands and clothing.

Every kit should have a veterinary check-up by the time he is nine weeks old, which should include his first permanent distemper vaccination and a stool test for parasites.

Remember that your kit is just a baby and needs to sleep a lot. Baby ferrets play very enthusiastically for an hour or so, then want to curl up for a nap. Especially for the first week you have him, allow him to do this whenever he wants to. He will be out of the baby stage in only a few weeks and then will have greater endurance than you do.

If you have cats or dogs with fleas, you can expect the ferret to get fleas, too. Try to get the other pets treated before you take the kit home. House him as far as possible from the cat or dog's favorite sleeping area, where most of the immature fleas will be waiting for a new host. A heavy burden of fleas can cause severe anemia in a small kit.

HOUSING

Ferrets are burrowing animals by nature and like to have a dark, private den-like place to sleep. If left on their own, they will choose a location for themselves, usually:

in a drawer - they can climb up the back of a dresser, get into the drawers, push them out one at a time,
    and eventually reach the top
inside an appliance
under a kitchen or bathroom cupboard
inside a piece of furniture
in a pile of clothing
in any box-like container with a lid on it
When providing a sleeping container in a cage, try to approximate what the ferret would choose.

Suggestions for ferret nests

Most ferrets like the commercial sleeping tubes that are available in some pet shops or in mail order catalogues. These are washable fabric tubes open at both ends so that several ferrets can get in at once, which is what they prefer to do. An approximation of a sleeping tube can be made from the sleeve of a sweatshirt or the leg of a pair of jogging pants. Some ferrets prefer sleeping in winter hats or wool socks.

Hammocks that attach to the cage wire are also popular: some of these have an imitation sheepskin lining.

Ferrets will arrange an ordinary terry hand towel over themselves to make a private nest.

Small plastic storage boxes are good ferret beds. Tie or clip them to the cage wire or the ferrets will move them around and tip them over.

Ferrets are gregarious by nature and like to sleep in a heap. Even when several beds are available in a cage of ferrets, they usually all sleep in one.

A type of clip used to fasten a litter box or nest box to the side of the ferret's cage.

Special conditions:

In warm summer months, ferrets should be housed in the coolest area possible, or in an air-conditioned room. They do not tolerate heat well and will die of heat stroke if left for more than a few minutes in a very warm area (over 90°F).

They can tolerate very cold temperatures if they are well fed and have a warm dry nest to sleep in. Traditionally ferrets have lived in outdoor cages raised off the ground, like rabbit hutches. This is a satisfactory arrangement if fresh water is supplied twice daily when temperatures are freezing, and their food is protected from moisture so that it stays fresh.

The major physical dangers of outdoor housing are neglect in inclement weather, escape of the ferret which may then be lost or accidentally killed, and infection with heartworms.

Small ferrets can escape if the cage wire is bigger than 1X1" mesh. Doors and openings for water or feed containers have to be very secure or the ferret will eventually dig his way out. Some feed hoppers meant for rabbits are big enough when empty that a small ferret can climb up and escape through the top opening.

In very warm weather, the cage should be in an area that is always shaded: even a few minutes in hot sun can kill a ferret. Fresh water should be offered twice a day in the hottest part of the summer.

FOR MORE INFORMATION ON . . .

spaying, neutering and descenting, see chapter 9

adrenal gland tumors, see chapter 16

ferret shows, see chapter 10

respiratory infections, see chapter 14

distemper, see chapter 15

chapter 6

WHAT TO FEED YOUR FERRET

Ferrets and cats are obligate carnivores (meat eaters). They cannot survive without meat in their diet. Dog food is inadequate for ferrets for two major reasons. First, obligate carnivores have special requirements for

several nutrients not included in dog foods. Second, ferrets are unable to digest the high levels of carbohydrate in dog food. They need to get most of their calories from simple carbohydrates, protein, and fat. Ferrets fed only dog food will eventually die of malnutrition. Pet ferrets should not be fed fresh raw meat. Although it is part of the natural diet of a carnivore, it often contains harmful parasites and microorganisms.

Until recently, high quality premium cat foods or diets for ranch mink or foxes were the only choices for feeding ferrets, other than preparing a ration at home by mixing cooked meats and other ingredients. Although ferrets do well on some mink and fox rations, these diets are sold in inconveniently large quantities and are not available everywhere.

Ferrets fed only dog food will die of malnutrition.

Now there are specially formulated ferret diets available at pet shops. Most of the original "ferret foods" were adapted from rations for mink, which have very similar requirements. The major dietary difference between mink and ferrets is that mink naturally eat fish, and ferrets do not. Fish is a major ingredient in all commercial mink rations. Some companies use poorly processed frozen fish that give the pellets a flavor unacceptable to many ferrets. These pellets are very dark colored and if wet, have a distinctly fishy smell. Kits that are offered this food at weaning will usually eat it and do well on it, but older ferrets accustomed to other diets often refuse to even taste it, and will starve if offered no other food. The newer ferret diets are formulated with palatability as well as nutritional balance in mind.

Premium quality cat foods sold in pet shops and veterinary clinics are not formulated specifically for ferrets, but most of them are palatable and all of them are nutritionally adequate for pet ferrets. Generic cat foods, sold in grocery and farm supply stores, are NOT good for ferrets. Generic cat foods cost less than premium foods, but they are too low in fat. The ferret has to eat at least twice as much of the cheaper food to get the calories he needs. There are some other important nutritional deficiencies in generic cat foods. It is a false economy to buy them for ferrets.

Ferrets, like some cats, become hooked on a particular flavor or brand of food and are very hard to change, even if the diet they prefer is nutritionally inadequate. It is important to start your young ferret on a good diet that is not likely to become unavailable in the future. The best insurance is to feed a mixture of several kinds of premium quality ferret and cat foods, so that the ferret adjusts to a variety of flavors, and does not insist on one. If one food is temporarily unavailable, the

Generic cat foods are palatable to most ferrets, but are nutritionally inadequate and lead to health problems.

ferret will be accustomed to the other ingredients of his diet and will not notice a big change. Anytime you have to drastically change the diet of a ferret, diarrhea and other digestive upsets are likely to follow. The more gradually a change in diet is made, the less upsetting it will be.

HOW YOU SHOULD FEED YOUR FERRET

Ferrets have such a short intestinal tract they can't eat very much at a time, and therefore need a concentrated diet. They should get most of the calories in their diet from fat, the most concentrated source of energy.

The best way to feed ferrets is to always leave dry food with them. Moist food sours after a few hours, especially in warm weather. This is one of the advantages of a dry diet. Convenience and keeping quality are other advantages, plus the beneficial effect crunchy food has on the ferret's teeth. Ferrets on moist diets develop much more plaque on their teeth sooner than ferrets on the same food fed dry.

Ferrets like to dig their food out of the container, especially if it is filled to the top. The best way to prevent this is to use a deep crockery bowl, or a plastic dish clipped high enough on the side of the cage to make it awkward for the ferret to dig in it. An adult female requires only about a quarter of a cup of food daily, so there is no need to fill the container very full. If you have multiple ferrets, it is better to use several dishes than to try to leave enough food in a single large container.

Ferrets on dry diets have to have a constant supply of water. The volume of water required is about three times the volume of dry pellets eaten. In warm weather they drink much more than usual. Ferrets that can't drink won't eat. Water bottles are a convenient way to keep clean water available, but ferrets prefer to drink from a dish and will drink much more from a dish than from a bottle. A dish of fresh water can be clipped onto the side of the cage, or made available to the ferrets when they get out for exercise. Kits and juveniles will usually play in a dish of water left on the cage floor, contaminating it with food and litter.

Proper storage of food is important. Pellets are packaged to protect them from moisture. When the bag is opened, it is your responsibility to do this. Store pelleted food no more than 3 months, even in an unopened bag. If you have only one ferret, you will have to buy small packages of food. These are more expensive than bulk quantities, but the food will be fresh and free of mold. Some ferret foods are packaged in milk-carton type containers that seal quite well after opening. Store the contents of large opened bags in plastic bins with snug-fitting lids. Bags of food should never be left in a basement or garage, where they will get damp and eventually moldy. Molds make the food unpalatable, and may produce toxins that can make animals very sick, or occasionally cause death.

Dry food and water should always be available to your pet ferret.

SNACKS

Ferrets don't need snacks, but owners sometimes need to feel good about themselves by giving their pet a treat. Treats can also be a useful training aid.

Nutritional problems arise when owners give ferrets the wrong kinds of food as treats. Sugary snacks can cause problems: ferrets have been known to develop diabetes and tooth decay when fed sugary treats every day. Dairy products, although very palatable to ferrets and nutritionally beneficial, cause diarrhea that can be distressing to the owner. Remember some fruits such as raisins, a favorite treat for many ferrets, contain large amounts of sugar. Ferrets may become so passionately fond of certain flavors that they won't eat anything else. Most snack foods are not well balanced. Overindulgence produces malnutrition and obesity.

Good snacks for ferrets, in limited quantities, include:
commercially packaged semi-moist cat or ferret treats, especially liver flavor
raisins (a few a day)
bananas (a small slice once a day)
milk (but see above)
Nutrical or other commercial nutritional cat supplements
linoleic acid coat conditioners (e.g., Linotone or Ferretone, a few drops a day)

Avoid marshmallows, potato chips, peanut butter, ice cream and soft drinks.

FOR MORE INFORMATION ON . . .

how to select a good diet for your ferret, see chapter 12

chapter 7

SOCIALIZING YOUR FERRET

SAFE TOYS FOR FERRETS

Ferret toys should be selected to give the pet enjoyment without endangering his life. Ferrets love to chew rubber. It is the most common cause of intestinal obstruction. Baby nipples and pacifiers are very attractive to ferrets, especially if they have any milk or formula on them. Both cats and ferrets will chew the end off a baby nipple, usually becoming obstructed and requiring surgery to remove the rubber from the intestine. Remove anything made of rubber from the ferret's play area. This includes the rubber coasters made to protect hardwood floors and rugs from the pressure of chair and table legs: even when the coasters are in use, some ferrets will gnaw pieces off them. Rubber dog and baby toys, rubber tubing, rubber or latex gloves, and rubber or plastic sandals are tempting snacks for ferrets.

Suitable ferret toys:
- ♥ fabric covered cat toys
- ♥ knotted cotton rope intended for dogs
- ♥ socks tied in a knot
- ♥ ferret balls, large plastic balls with holes cut in them so ferrets can get inside and roll around: these are commercially available
- ♥ empty milk jugs with holes cut in them
- ♥ empty paper bags, the bigger the better
- ♥ cardboard boxes with small holes cut in the sides so ferrets can climb in and out
- ♥ pvc tubing (plastic sewer pipe) or similar tunnel-like materials
- ♥ cardboard mailing tubes big enough to get inside
- ♥ waste baskets containing smaller items of interest
- ♥ a dish pan containing a little water and a lot of newspaper spread around it (not all ferrets like to play in water but those that do are very entertaining)
- ♥ "stolen" items such as shoes, socks, gloves or mitts, slippers, hats, car keys
- ♥ other ferrets
- ♥ other animals trained as ferret playmates, such as cats and dogs
- ♥ people who like ferrets, especially those sweeping the floor, reading a newspaper, or doing other interesting tasks to attract ferret "help"

Most ferrets will chew and swallow rubber or latex.

Most ferrets have a favorite place to hide their treasures. Watch where they go so you will know where to look for your missing treasures when they vanish.

TRAINING YOUR FERRET

Ferrets are hard to train compared to dogs because they are not concerned about pleasing you, they like to please themselves. They also have a very short attention span for anything they don't think of themselves. When first let out to play, they are so excited and active they pay no attention to anything.

The only very useful trick is coming when called. This will save a lot of time and anxiety searching for the ferret, or trying to extract him from small spaces if he gets out of his usual play area. Train him by rewarding him every time he obeys. The best reward is a

Expensive toys are not a necessity. A cardboard "playhouse" is safe and interesting for ferrets.

favorite food. Most ferrets like chicken or liver flavored semi-moist treats, and all ferrets love Ferretone or Linotone. The advantage to the semi-moist treats is that you can shake the box when you call the ferret, and train him to come to the sound of the rattle. You could use some other sound to go with the Ferretone treat. If you are consistent, the ferret will quickly associate the sound and the treat, and come running from wherever he is.

Before you start trying to train a ferret to do anything, allow him to slow down after his initial exuberant play, because he will not learn much until he can pay attention. Always take him to the same area for his lessons, preferably away from distractions or other ferrets, and he will learn to associate both the place and the sound of the treat container with a pleasant experience. The most important lesson is coming when called, but people have taught ferrets to sit up, roll over, fetch things, and more theatrical tricks by using this simple method.

LITTER TRAINING

Ferrets are clean by nature. Adults will avoid soiling their beds or eating areas, although kits are not so fastidious. Ferrets naturally back into corners with their tails raised to urinate or defecate, and usually do both at the same time. Because they have such a short intestine, they feel the need to empty it more frequently than other pets.

Confine a newly acquired kit to its cage except when it is out for exercise and play with human observation. Provide a litter box in the cage, plus a nest such as a sleeping tube or hammock, and a dish or hopper for food. For the first few days, the kit will back into any corner when it needs to relieve itself. If you're there, you can pick it up when you see this behavior, and put it into the corner of the litter box. Kits often think the litter is a wonderful play area and will enthusiastically dig and burrow in it for the first week after adoption. They will get over this when they begin to understand what the litter box is for. Kits that are slow learners should be given a litter box that is at least half the area of the cage floor, so that they just about can't avoid using the litter box without fouling their bed or food. At least one side should be low enough that the kit doesn't have to climb over more than an inch to get in.

When you wake your pet for playtime, don't take him out of the cage until he uses the litter box. The first thing he will do when you let him out, unless you give him a chance to relieve himself, will be to use the nearest corner for that purpose. Stay with the kit while he is out and whenever you see him start to back into a corner, put him in the litterbox. You may want to provide several boxes in the room so that the kit will find one when he is some distance from the cage. It doesn't take long for a ferret to decide which corners he prefers, and he will train you to provide litter areas in those spots. Some owners allow their pets to use paper in the corners, especially if the ferrets have their own room with a washable floor. The most important thing to remember is that animals learn by repetition, and you cannot expect good results unless you spend time with the ferret when he is young, reinforcing the behavior you prefer.

Litter boxes for cats are too high for young ferrets. They need to be cut down until a space on one side is no more than an inch high. There are special litter boxes made for ferrets, with a low side and a guard on the higher edges to prevent the animal backing far enough up to miss the box. Ferrets do not cover their stool, so only a thin layer of litter is needed. If more is put in, many ferrets will dig it out.

There are three types of litter available: regular clay litter, fine clumping litter, and several types of wood products. The wood products include pellets of recycled paper, shredded paper, and fine cedar shavings. Some litter contains odor controlling substances such as baking soda and perfume. Occasional ferrets and cats object to the perfume, and will suddenly stop using the box when you introduce a perfumed litter. Some clumping litters and coarse clay litters are very dusty and can cause sneezing, especially when young kits dig and burrow in it. Shredded paper is very hard to handle when it becomes wet and makes it difficult to keep the box clean. Litter made from recycled paper is very good for ferrets. It is not dusty, has no odor of its own, is very absorptive, and is easy to handle. Cedar litter has a faint cedar smell that does not appear to bother ferrets, and discourages fleas from entering the cage. It is also possible just to put folded newspaper in the corners of the cage and rooms that the ferrets will live in, and change it frequently.

Three kinds of litter suitable for ferrets: paper pellets, dust-free clumpable cat litter and finely chopped wood chips (this is cedar).

CONTROLLING LOOSE HAIR

Ferrets require little grooming. They lick themselves and may develop hairballs in their stomachs during the spring and fall, when they shed their coats. Brushing with a soft brush or cat grooming mitt helps get rid of loose hair, especially when a fluffy winter coat is being shed. Treat at least once weekly during the shedding period with a malt-based cat or ferret laxative. Ferrets find these products very palatable and cooperate in eating the laxative from the tube.

Most ferrets will readily eat malt-based laxatives from the tube

CONTROLLING FERRET ODOR

Some people find the innate odor of the ferret offensive. In breeding season, uncastrated males and females in heat have a very pungent body odor. Spayed or neutered animals have only a faint ferret odor. Descenting does nothing to change ferret body odor. The musk glands produce a secretion with a strong, unpleasant odor different from the typical ferret scent. Most kits

To bathe your ferret without causing dry, itchy skin, use a baby shampoo or, preferably a special shampoo made for ferrets or cats. Be sure to rinse it off thoroughly.

sold in pet shops are both descented and spayed or neutered when sold. When these kits are adopted, the odor associated with them can be controlled by keeping them and their environment clean. Keeping the cage and litter box clean minimizes ferret muskiness. The sleeping tube or bedding should be washed once a week. Ferrets do not bury waste in the litter; it should be cleaned out once or twice a day.

Very fastidious people bathe their ferret once a week. There is some danger of causing dry, itchy skin with frequent baths. Use very gentle products such as baby shampoo, never dish-washing detergents. There are special ferret shampoos and coat conditioners on the market. You can also use shampoos and conditioners formulated for cats. If fleas are a problem use a cat flea shampoo, or follow the regular shampoo with a flea dip. Ferrets should always be shampooed before a flea dip to remove the oil from the hair and allow the dip to penetrate to the skin, where the fleas live.

BATHING A FERRET

To give the ferret a bath, fill a basin or sink half full of warm water, wet the ferret, put a generous stream of shampoo down his back, then lather him all over. A small dab of vaseline around the eyes and at the entrance to the ears will prevent water and soap from entering.

When giving a flea bath, thoroughly treat the head and face, or the fleas that escape the body will congregate there. A flea dip must also be applied to the face and ears, preferably using a sponge to control

Ferrets may initially be alarmed when soaked with warm water and lathered with shampoo, but most learn to submit if held firmly and not frightened by the first bath.

the amount of liquid flowing over the face. Any dip that is safe for a cat is safe for a ferret when mixed according to the directions on the container. Flea dips labeled for dogs only are not safe for cats and may not be safe for ferrets. Flea dips should be the final rinse: they should not be followed by a rinse of clear water or most of the residual action will be lost. Ferrets dry very quickly after being wrapped in a towel to remove the excess water. Most like to run around after their bath and dry themselves on rugs and furniture. Unless the ferret is very young or old or is sick, there is no need to put it in an extra warm place to dry.

EAR CARE

Ferrets produce a lot of ear wax normally, and when they are infested with ear mites this will be in larger quantities and will be dark red. Ferrets rarely scratch or shake their heads even when their ears are full of wax: you will have to inspect the ears to know when they need cleaning. Ordinarily, ferrets will not require ear cleaning unless they have mites, although some older hobs secrete a great deal of wax that builds up both on the skin and inside the ears.

Occasionally ferrets get ear infections. This can result from the following conditions: secondary to the damage done by ear mites; after exposure to another animal with an ear infection; after a bath that has allowed water to get into the ear.

Ferrets with ear infections will both scratch and shake their heads, and the discharge will be brown, yellow or green pus that may have a bad odor.

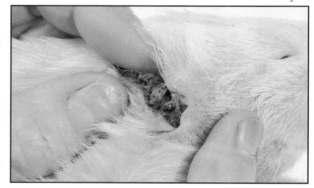

Dark red wax like this means ear mites.

SCRUFFING

Ferrets won't allow you to do anything to their ears without firm restraint. This means scruffing the ferret. It is easiest if one person scruffs the ferret and a second person treats the ears.

Scruffing means taking a firm hold on the loose skin of the nape of the neck, and gathering it into a bunch so that the facial skin is stretched tightly enough to make the eyes squinty. This prevents the ferret from turning and twisting around, and seems to put it into a trance for a short time. Most ferrets will hang limply from your hand. If held that way for a few minutes they will yawn, sometimes repeatedly. When scruffed, even ferrets that don't bite will close their jaws firmly on anything that goes into their mouths, so keep your fingers out.

"Scruffing" means grasping a good handful of neck skin and suspending the ferret. Notice how relaxed this jill has become, making ear-cleaning and nail trimming a quick procedure.

CLEAN THE EAR

Ferrets have very small ear canals. There is little value in putting medication on a thick layer of discharge. Do not put cotton-tipped applicators into the ear canal to remove wax: it will just be pushed further down, and may injure the eardrum. Your veterinarian can dispense an ear cleaning solution. After putting a few drops of this solution into the ear, massage it to soften and loosen material far down in the ear canal, and bring it up to the surface. A cotton-tipped swab can be used to clean this off the outer part of the ear. Repeat this as often as necessary to get the ear canal very clean before using any medication.

TREAT THE EAR FOR EAR MITES

Drop the ear mite medication into the ear canal: a large quantity is not necessary but it should go well down into the canal, not sit on the surface of the external ear. Treatment must be repeated several times at regular intervals to kill all the mites. The length of the intervals will depend on the specific medication. If there are either cats or dogs in the same area as the ferret, treat all of them for mites or the ferret will become reinfested very soon.

CHECK FOR EAR INFECTIONS

If your ferret has red, sore-looking ears, it probably has a bacterial or yeast infection and should be taken to a veterinarian for treatment. Ear infections can take a long time to completely clear up, especially if they are neglected or incorrectly treated to begin with. Take the ferret to a veterinarian if you have treated it for ear mites and the ears are still red and sore, or have a constant discharge that looks like pus instead of wax. Sometimes a bacterial culture of the ear is required to decide what type of antibiotic will work best.

NAIL TRIMMING

Ferrets have non-retractable claws. They do not sharpen them like cats. They should NEVER be declawed. They do use their claws to dig holes in anything they want moved, such as bedding, litter, carpets, furniture stuffing or soil in potted plants. When the nails get very long, they will catch in fabrics and cause the ferret to injure itself, or cause scratches on people who play with the animal.

Nails need to be trimmed about once a month, depending on the surface the ferret usually walks and plays on and how much digging he does in substances that will wear the nails down. Human nail clippers work well for ferrets, and there are small, scissor-like trimmers made especially for ferrets. The nails are always transparent. They should be trimmed only enough to blunt them, avoiding the pink area at the base. If a nail is clipped too short, it will hurt and may bleed. This won't do any serious harm and will not need any special treatment if it happens, but the ferret will protest more the next time nails need to be trimmed.

RESTRAINT FOR NAIL TRIMMING

It is difficult to restrain a ferret long enough to do all the nails at one sitting unless an attractive diversion is provided. Linoleic acid products (such as Ferretone or Linotone) are very palatable to ferrets. Put a few drops on the ferret's belly, or on the hand that is holding the paw being trimmed. The ferret will lick enthusiastically, barely noticing the procedure taking place. Alternatively, if there is an extra set of hands available, the ferret can be scruffed by one person and the second person can do the trimming. The advantage of the Linotone method is that the ferret learns to enjoy the procedure because of the treat and becomes easier to manage.

Avoid the pink area of the nail and cut off only the sharp curved tip.

FOR MORE INFORMATION ON . . .

ear mites and fleas, see chapter 13

descenting see chapter 9

Schedule of veterinary care for baby ferrets

6 to 9 weeks old
- first veterinary visit to assess general health
- stool sample to check for intestinal parasites

9 or 10 weeks
- first distemper vaccination

12 or 13 weeks
- second distemper vaccination
- rabies vaccination

14 to 16 weeks
- third distemper vaccination

VETERINARY CARE FOR ADULT FERRETS

All ferrets should be vaccinated for distemper and rabies once a year, even if they don't go outside. People who contact dogs or walk in a place where an infected dog has urinated can carry distemper to the ferret. Exposure to rabies is rare but because it is a fatal disease in man, it is your responsibility to take every possible precaution to protect your pet and people who contact it.

Some ferrets are allergic to distemper or rabies vaccines. Ferrets that are allergic show a reaction known as anaphylaxis. Within minutes of being vaccinated, the ferret begins vomiting, and may also have diarrhea. Some go limp and may lose consciousness. Ferrets that have this reaction once will not necessarily have another when vaccinated again. It is wise to remain at the veterinary office for 15 minutes after an injection is given to a ferret that once reacted to a vaccine. There is a treatment that works rapidly to reverse the reaction. It is not worth the risk of

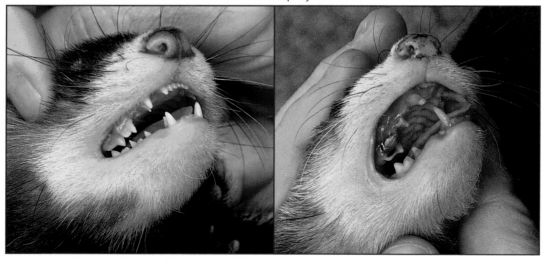

Compare the normal teeth on the left to those on the right, which have accumulated a great deal of plaque and need immediate attention. The 9-week-old kit on the left is still teething. Notice he has both baby and permanent canine teeth.

leaving the ferret unvaccinated. Ferrets rarely die of the allergic reaction, but many unvaccinated ferrets die of distemper. Some veterinarians dispense a dose of antihistamine to owners of ferrets that have had a reaction to a vaccine. This is given an hour before the ferret is to be vaccinated, and prevents the allergic reaction from taking place.

Ferrets that live outside or are taken outside during summer months should be put on heartworm prevention when the mosquito season starts, or year-round in the southern US. The medication must be prescribed by a veterinarian.

Ferrets eventually develop plaque on their teeth. If this is removed at regular intervals, the teeth will remain healthy. Your veterinarian can check your ferret's teeth when he is scheduled for vaccinations.

As ferrets age, they become susceptible to several kinds of cancer such as insulinomas, tumors in the pancreas that cause low blood sugar (hypoglycemia). Insulinomas diagnosed and removed early are less likely to spread to other parts of the body. Early diagnosis reduces the chance that the ferret will someday become severely hypoglycemic when you're not with him, and possibly die before you can treat him. Mild hypoglycemia can be detected by a blood test before the ferret has shown signs of illness. A ferret over three years old should have an annual blood glucose test. Blood tests can also reveal a high white cell count, that might mean leukemia, or a high BUN, suggesting a kidney problem.

A veterinary check-up once a year can reveal other problems such as ear mites, fleas, abnormal hair loss, bladder infections, blindness, and abdominal masses, that may be reversible with early treatment.

WHAT ABOUT SPAYING OR NEUTERING?

Jills are induced ovulators, meaning that they remain in heat (estrus) indefinitely unless ovulation is induced by breeding. All female pet ferrets should be spayed to avoid the following health problems caused by side effects of being in heat for more than three weeks: loss of hair and body weight, bladder infections, bladder stones, and bone marrow failure causing anemia, internal hemorrhage and death.

Spaying is removal of both the ovaries and uterus of the female. The surgery can be done any time after weaning. Ferrets tolerate anesthetics well and are fast healers. They show no signs of pain after surgery.

Males have a very strong body odor and greasy skin secretion during the breeding season (early spring to mid-summer). Few pet owners would choose to tolerate the smell of a male ferret in breeding condition in their homes.

Male ferrets in breeding condition are rarely aggressive with human beings. However, they will usually attack other male ferrets, biting them around the head and neck. These skirmishes rarely do serious harm but will leave sore spots where they bite and hang on to the neck and ears. The wounds take a long time to heal and the hair may never grow normally again. Intact (uncastrated) males should always be housed individually. Male ferrets reach their full stature, but not their full weight, and become sexually mature by 8 months of age. Depending on the season of the year, they may then start trying to breed any females that they encounter, in heat or not, and fight with other intact or neutered males. Because of this behavior, you may choose to have them neutered a bit earlier than eight months of age.

A mature hob in breeding condition has a strong body odor and very greasy skin, staining the white hair yellow in this Albino.

Neutering, or castration, is removal of both testicles, which are the source of the male hormones that produce the ferret odor. The side effects of neutering a male ferret include loss of greasy skin secretion and odor, slimming of the head and neck area, and behavioral changes. Ferrets castrated before sexual maturity do not grow as large as animals neutered later in life. Much of the difference in size between male and female ferrets is due to the growth-stimulating effect of male hormones.

WHAT DIFFERENCE DOES DESCENTING MAKE?

Descenting is a surgical procedure to remove the anal sacs, which are musk-producing glands on either side of the anal opening. Descenting alone does nothing to change ferret body odor. The musk secretion has a very pungent odor of its own but is secreted only when the ferret is startled or frightened.

All carnivores have anal sacs that produce a strong smelling secretion with a distinctive odor for each species. The anal gland secretion of mustelids, particularly skunks, is more pungent than that of other carnivores. The contents of the sacs are released as a defense against attackers, most effectively by skunks.

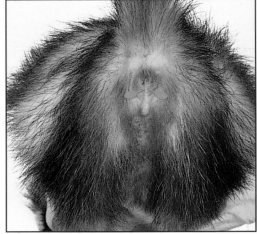

Properly handled pet ferrets will rarely discharge the contents of their anal sacs, because they never feel sufficiently threatened. This defense is most likely to be triggered when the ferret is physically attacked by another ferret or a larger animal. Although the odor of ferret glands is very strong, it dissipates completely in a short time. Descenting is not absolutely necessary for a ferret to be a good house pet. Pet shop ferrets are usually descented when they are spayed or neutered.

It is best to descent ferrets when they are only 6 to 8 weeks old. The surgery becomes more difficult and more traumatic as the ferret gets older and fatter. Descenting incisions in young animals are usually not stitched and heal completely in 2 or 3 days without causing the kit any distress.

Descenting means surgical removal of the scent glands, which open, as shown, on the anal sphincter.

Occasionally young kits have a prolapsed rectum, indicated by protrusion of bright pink tissue from the anal opening. This has been attributed to the descenting surgery, but rectal prolapses also occur in kits that have not had the surgery. It may be due to the weaning process, when kits suddenly eat only dry food without the laxative effect of milk. Firmer, drier stool causes mild straining that may induce a temporary rectal prolapse, that usually disappears without treatment.

TEETH AND TEETHING

Ferrets are carnivores and have sharp teeth for tearing meat and crunching bones. They cut the first of their 30 baby teeth when they are less than three weeks old. At this age, their eyes and ear canals are not open, and they are still almost helpless and totally dependent on their mother for food and warmth. At three to four weeks old, they begin to eat solid food if they have access to it.

Ferrets' 34 permanent teeth are similar to cats' teeth in appearance. The permanent teeth can be used to estimate the age of a young ferret. The large pointed teeth at the front of the mouth are called canines. These erupt when the kit is between seven and eight weeks old. The last teeth to erupt are the lower back molars, when the ferret is about 10 weeks old. A ferret with permanent canine teeth but some baby teeth remaining is 8 to 10 weeks old.

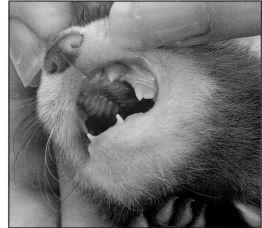

Some ferrets have inherited tooth problems. They may have short noses ("pug" faces) and associated with this have crooked teeth, because there is not enough room in their mouths for the normal number of teeth. Most commonly, the lower canine teeth stick out. This is not harmful unless the teeth press against the lips, which they often do, causing a sore spot. Occasionally even ferrets that have normally pointed noses have canine teeth that grow at unusual angles. When selecting a pet, avoid kits that have these

A 7-week-old kit with only baby teeth.

problems, because it will mean removing or grinding down the permanent canines later. Grinding the teeth is not recommended because there is a sensitive area in the center of the tooth that will be exposed. Extracting healthy canine teeth without fracturing the jaw is difficult. The best way to avoid the problem is not to buy or breed ferrets with this characteristic.

Ferrets fed a soft diet are more likely to have a significant build-up of calculus and plaque (tartar) on the teeth than those fed a dry pelleted ration. Ferrets over three years of age should have their teeth cleaned to remove plaque, to avoid early periodontal disease and loss of teeth. Check your ferret's teeth, especially the canine teeth and upper molars, to see how much plaque has accumulated. Your veterinarian will check these teeth when the ferret has its annual vaccinations, and can recommend cleaning when it is required. Cleaning means giving the ferret a general anesthetic and using steel scrapers or an ultrasonic scaler to loosen and remove the plaque. This might have to be done once or twice a year in older ferrets, depending on the condition of the teeth and the diet.

These protruding teeth press on the lips and can cause open sores that do not heal.

MY FERRET IS GOING BALD!

Photoperiod, the number of hours of light per 24-hour period, greatly affects ferrets. The most obvious effect is molting. Every spring the ferret will shed out its fluffy winter coat, and grow a sleeker new one. In the fall, the summer coat is changed for a winter one. The ferret will lose weight in the spring, and gain it in the fall, preparing for winter. Hair loss is usually gradual, but some ferrets shed their whole coat overnight, leaving them with almost no hair for several days. Sometimes the guard hairs (the longer surface hair with the distinctive color) come out first, leaving only the woollier, pale yellow undercoat. The hair may come out in patches, giving the ferret a moth-eaten appearance. This is normal and within days shiny new short hair can be seen coming up through the undercoat.

Some ferrets lose most or all of the hair on their tail every summer. This phenomenon, called tail alopecia, is most common in males. The tail begins to look like a rat's tail, with scaly skin, sparse, bristly hair, and blackheads. This is a very unattractive but harmless occurrence with no known cause. Many nutritional, medical and dermatological remedies have been tried, and sometimes the hair grows back, with or without treatment. Usually when the ferret changes his coat in the fall, the tail hair regrows, but he is likely to lose it again the next spring.

Tail alopecia: this jill has almost no hair on her tail every summer, but it regrows when she gets her winter coat.

Hair loss caused by hormonal imbalance has a distinct pattern. The hair thins at the base of the tail and inside the legs first, then gradually is lost over most of the body, often sparing the tip of the tail and the head. The common causes are adrenal gland tumors and prolonged heat periods. Jills in heat will grow the hair back when they go out of heat or are spayed. Ferrets with adrenal tumors will develop other more serious problems. If your ferret is spayed, and begins to show hair loss in the described pattern, take her to a veterinarian.

Because the ferret's coat is so sensitive to photoperiod, it may not grow in for a long time after being clipped for surgery or other medical treatment. If the ferret is in a rapid hair growth phase, as in early winter or late spring, the hair will regrow completely in only a few days. If the skin is shaved at other times, such as mid-summer, the area may remain hairless for weeks or months. Just before the hair of dark-colored ferrets begins to come in, the skin will turn black or dark blue, alarming owners who haven't seen this happen before. It is just a sign that the hair follicles are making hair pigment, and it will be only a few days before the new coat is evident.

This jill's coat is sparse because she has been in heat a long time. Endocrine alopecia can also be caused by an adrenal gland tumor.

ITCHY FERRETS

Ferrets often scratch when they first wake up. If you sleep near your pets, you can hear the rattle of cage wire when they get up during the night and scratch vigorously. However, if a ferret spends a lot of its time scratching, there is something wrong.

Fleas are a common cause of itching. The best place to check for fleas is between the shoulder blades. There may be flea bites and raw red patches in this area, and thinning of the hair. The skin will need no other treatment than to get rid of the fleas.

Frequent baths with harsh shampoos or failure to rinse the shampoo off thoroughly after a bath cause dry, itchy skin. The treatment for this is to give another bath with a mild shampoo followed by a cream rinse. There are ferret shampoos and rinses on the market that are mild enough to use frequently, but it is important, no matter how mild the shampoo, to rinse until the hair is squeaky clean.

Occasionally ferrets develop allergies and will be itchy whenever they contact the offending substances. This is much less common than in dogs and cats. Food allergies cause whole body itching. Generic cat foods that contain ingredients such as soybeans and dyes may cause allergies in both cats and ferrets. Sensitivity to rugs or other materials will usually cause the worst reaction at the most frequent points of contact, for instance the feet. When medications such as ear mite treatment cause hypersensitivity or allergy, only the treated areas are affected. The obvious remedy is to eliminate the offending substance.

Ferrets on poor diets, too low in animal fats, will have dry lusterless coats and itchy skin. Changing to a better diet will solve the problem. Giving a linoleic acid supplement daily for a week while the diet is being changed will return the skin to health more rapidly.

Ferrets housed outside or in contact with mangy dogs can get sarcoptic mange, which usually affects the feet and legs first, causing raw, red weeping areas. This is uncommon in pet ferrets housed indoors.

Older ferrets (over 4 years old) may be itchy all over with no sign of any skin irritation, but show other signs of abnormality. They may have hair loss around the rear quarters or over their entire body. They may be lethargic and less playful than usual. Females may have a very swollen vulva, as though they were in heat, even if they are spayed. These signs are caused by an adrenal gland tumor. When the tumor is removed, all signs, including the itchiness, will be resolved.

FIRST AID FOR FERRETS

Some ferret emergencies require immediate attention by a veterinarian, but there are things you can do on the way to the clinic to improve the chances that your pet will survive. Other emergencies can be taken care of at home by an alert and calm owner.

Heat stroke

Ferrets that get too hot because of environmental temperature, or when left near a heat source too long, will start to breathe through their mouths. They will collapse and die if confined at temperatures over 90°F for 10 minutes. If you find your ferret panting, remove it from the hot area immediately. If possible, lay it flat on its belly on a cement floor or a dry bathtub; these surfaces are always cool and the ferret will improve quickly. Alternatively, fill a sink with tepid water (NOT COLD) and submerge the ferret, supporting his body just below the surface, until he is soaking wet. He can then be put near a fan or in a breeze, and will cool off quickly. Don't try to force-feed cold water, the ferret may inhale it and will choke. Allow free access to water when the ferret can walk.

Hypoglycemia

Hypoglycemia means low blood sugar. The muscles and brain depend on blood sugar (glucose) for energy. Severe hypoglycemia is life-threatening. It causes weakness and mental confusion, progressing to convulsions and coma. Hypoglycemia occurs in ferrets that have insulin-producing pancreatic tumors (insulinomas), or that have been accidentally starved, particularly babies or pregnant jills. Occasionally ferrets on oral antibiotics such as amoxicillin

A ferret that frequently drops into this crouched position might just be "spacey" by nature, or may be having hypoglycemic attacks.

will become hypoglycemic. The signs are the same whatever the cause. Ferrets first look confused or "spacey,"and lie on their bellies with their heads up, staring blankly around as though they were blind or deaf. Normal ferrets will sometimes drop flat on the floor after a wildly active play session, but they get up and go back to their activity after a short rest. Hypoglycemic ferrets move very slowly and respond poorly to activity nearby. Some salivate and paw at their mouths. Eventually they will lose consciousness and convulse. If your ferret has an attack of hypoglycemia, he should have an appointment with a veterinarian to find the cause.

Meanwhile, you should treat him yourself because you are the closest person and time is important. Owners will learn to recognize the early signs and treat the ferret with a concentrated sugar, such as corn syrup or liquid honey, to relieve the condition before it becomes severe. The sugar should be followed by a high protein and fat snack, because sugar induces more insulin production and a second attack of hypoglycemia.

Respiratory infections

Ferrets with colds or flu have runny noses that may be completely blocked with discharge. They can neither breathe nor eat when this happens. Wipe the nose with a tissue. If there is a lot more discharge inside, put the ferret in a steamy bathroom or in a small room with a baby vaporizer until the mucus is softened and can be wiped away. Put a small amount of vaseline around the nostrils to help prevent the secretion drying again. Moisten the ferret's regular pellets with water and microwave it. Warming brings out the flavor and odor to tempt him to eat. Ferrets that refuse to eat even after their noses are cleared, or that have large amounts of thick yellow or green nasal discharge, will probably need antibiotics and should visit a veterinarian.

If your house is very dry, get a humidifier for the ferret's living space. Don't keep him in the warmest area of the house, which will be stressful for him. Keep him in a cool area and provide a warm nest for sleeping. The cage and litter box should be kept extra clean to avoid irritating ammonia fumes. If there is a smoker in the house the ferret's quarters should be protected from the smoke.

Diarrhea

Ferrets that have watery diarrhea will become dehydrated in a few hours and require veterinary care. If you cannot get to a veterinarian, get some Pedialyte, an electrolyte solution made for human infants and sold in grocery stores. Give the ferret as much as you can get him to swallow, by scruffing him and gently dripping the fluid into the corner of his mouth with a plastic eye dropper. As a rough estimate, the ferret will need 10% of his body weight (measured in grams) in balanced electrolytes (measured in ml's) to replace fluid lost in watery diarrhea. An average jill weighs 700 to 800 grams, and needs 70 to 80 ml of electrolytes per day (28 ml= 1 oz). A male needs about twice as much.

Ferrets that are very dehydrated feel "doughy"; their skin doesn't slide along their bodies as it usually does, and if you pinch a fold of it, the fold will stay there when you let go. Their eyes are dull and often half closed. Ferrets in this condition need injectable electrolytes very soon or they will die.

Ferrets with very soft but not watery stool might not require any treatment, depending on circumstances. If soft stool is caused by a dietary change, you can control the ferret's intake until the problem resolves. If soft stool continues for more than a day, particularly if it contains mucus or blood, take the ferret to a veterinarian. Meanwhile, remove from the diet foods such as dairy products, that induce diarrhea. Cat laxatives given in large quantities can induce severe diarrhea and should also be withheld until the stool is normal. Drinking water should be provided in a dish to make sure the ferret gets all he needs. Make no drastic food changes until the stool returns to normal.

Vomiting

Ferrets that suddenly stop eating and vomit once or twice, producing little but mucus or froth, usually have hairballs. If the ferret seems to feel quite well when you notice the vomiting, give him several inches of cat laxative. If he does not eat and begins to look sick, take him to a veterinarian. He may have swallowed some other type of foreign body, or he may just need more laxative, but he should have professional help in case the problem is serious. If one dose of laxative hasn't started the ferret eating normally but he seems to feel well, repeat the dose and wait overnight. Usually two big doses of laxative will move hairballs. Check the litterbox: when the hair starts to pass, you can see it in the stool. If there are no results from two or three treatments, even if the ferret doesn't look very sick, take him to your veterinarian for diagnosis of the problem.

Prolapsed rectum

Ferrets that have diarrhea sometimes strain until the soft pink lining of the rectum is pushed through the anal opening. This is common in juvenile ferrets with proliferative colitis, a severe inflammation of the lower intestine. It happens sometimes in young kits soon after arrival at pet shops. Usually the cause is a change to a dry diet that the kits eat in large quantities because they're hungry after their long trip. It is rarely associated with descenting when the surgery is properly done in a young ferret. Occasionally, coccidiosis, a parasitic disease, causes bloody diarrhea and a prolapsed rectum in 6 to 10-week old kits. A prolapsed rectum is not an emergency unless the ferret feels so irritated that he begins to chew the prolapse, which can cause profuse hemorrhage. If a newly acquired kit has a small prolapse, give a half inch of cat laxative paste twice a day. The prolapse will often vanish spontaneously within 48 hours. Make sure the kit has water available and consider feeding him a soft diet for a few days, by mixing his pellets with warm water. A ferret with severe diarrhea causing prolapsed rectum should be seen by a veterinarian as soon as possible.

WHAT TO KEEP IN YOUR FERRET'S MEDICINE CABINET

- palatable nutritional supplement in paste form (e.g., Nutrical)
- Ensure Plus or other human nutritional supplement
- corn syrup or liquid honey
- ferret or cat laxative in paste form
- linoleic acid liquid supplement (e.g., Ferretone, Linotone)
- ear mite treatment
- cat flea spray, dip or both
- ferret shampoo and conditioner
- nail trimmers
- plastic eye droppers

FOR MORE INFORMATION ON . . .

distemper and rabies, see chapter 15

heartworms, see chapter 13

reproduction, see chapter 11

adrenal gland tumors, see chapter 16

insulinomas, see chapter 16

respiratory infections, see chapter 14

diarrhea and vomiting, see chapter 14

coccidiosis, see chapter 13

chapter 10

GOING PLACES AND DOING THINGS

TRAVELING

Avoid travelling with your ferret if possible. There are several very good reasons for this advice.

Ferrets are so heat sensitive that a few minutes in a closed car or sitting in a cage on an airport dock in hot weather can kill them. People often underestimate the time they are away from their vehicle and find the ferret gasping for breath when they return.

Ferrets are escape artists. A ferret that gets out of your car, trailer or motel room will likely be killed by a vehicle, an animal, or a human, or may die of heat prostration or starvation.

Ferrets are often frightened, excited, or impatient to get moving when they are in unfamiliar surroundings. People cannot resist touching animals and may be bitten by a usually gentle ferret. Even if the bite doesn't break the skin, some people will panic and report the incident to the authorities. Most public health departments categorize ferrets as wild or exotic rather than as domestic animals, as far as rabies vaccination status is concerned. A rabies vaccinated dog or cat is quarantined if it bites someone, but the law does not distinguish between a vaccinated or unvaccinated exotic animal. Even a vaccinated ferret may be seized and killed for a rabies test. It is easier for all concerned to leave your ferret with a reliable house-sitter who is used to ferrets.

This type of kennel is suitable for ferrets traveling long distances. Smaller ones can be used for short trips in a car.

Ferrets may contact, directly or indirectly, diseases that can endanger their lives. Even vaccinated ferrets should be protected as much as possible from distemper and rabies. Influenza is common in airports and many ferrets that travel by air come down with respiratory infections soon afterwards. The viral diarrhea that appeared in show ferrets in 1993 spreads mainly by direct contact with infected ferrets, but also by the hands of people who touched them. A ferret that recovered from the disease but still carries the virus can indirectly infect other ferrets touched by his owner's hands.

Some states and some areas within states forbid keeping ferrets as pets. If your ferret is seen in a public place or if someone lodges a complaint, your pet could be seized, and there are other stiff penalties for defying these laws.

If you do decide to travel with your ferret:

Protect it at all costs from contact with people and other ferrets. Don't let strangers pet or handle your ferret, both to protect the ferret from diseases, and to prevent it taking the slightest nibble at someone's finger.

Carry it in a well-ventilated, securely fastened comfortable pet carrier.

NEVER leave it unattended in a car in summer months, even with the windows open.

If you take it anywhere on a leash, make sure the harness is secure and don't take your eyes off the ferret. Some ferrets can escape even from snugly adjusted figure-8 harnesses.

Make sure to take enough of the ferret's usual food: if it is not available where you are travelling your ferret may refuse to eat.

Take along a list of ferret shelters or clubs in the area where you will be staying. Local ferret associations can supply you with a list of veterinarians in their area who will treat ferrets in case something happens on your trip. They can also advise you of the availability of a specific kind of food or litter.

Some ferrets can squirm out of even the most securely fastened figure-8 harness. Don't take your eyes off your pet if you take him out on a leash, and never tie a ferret outside by itself.

Make sure the ferret's rabies and distemper vaccinations are up to date a week before you travel.

If your pet has any health problems, take along enough medication to last the trip, and take it in two separate containers if possible, to allow for loss or spillage of one.

If you insist on travelling in a state that forbids ferrets, keep your pet out of sight. If he is seen by someone who reports him to the authorities, he may pay for your vacation with his life.

BOARDING

If your ferret stays behind while you travel, the best place to leave it is in its own home. Neighbors or friends who own ferrets will usually take better care of the ferret than the average boarding kennel devoted primarily to caring for dogs and cats. In some areas there are "pet sitters" who will stop by your home and look after your animals as often as necessary. Check with local ferret organizations to see if there is someone in your area who specializes in ferret sitting. Some kennels will board ferrets and/or other exotic pets, and there are a few ferret boarding facilities in large cities. These people are often very knowledgeable and will do their best to keep your ferret safe and healthy.

Be sure to check the kennel before you decide to leave your ferret, to avoid the kinds of problems discussed below.

Problems with boarding facilities:

Most ferrets are not upset by barking dogs but if yours is, choose a kennel that is devoted to ferrets, cats, or exotics that don't make a lot of noise.

Not all boarding kennels will be careful to feed your pet the diet it is used to, even if you leave a supply with them. Caretakers find it easier to feed all the animals the same food and some believe that all cat food is created equal. Ferrets can be very choosy about what they eat and some go on a starvation diet when a new food is suddenly introduced. The food offered by the kennel might be palatable but not nutritious enough for a ferret. Ferrets tip stainless steel dishes over, spilling and contaminating the food and water, and making it hard to tell how much has been eaten.

Select a kennel that will reliably feed your pet the food you leave for it. They should allow you to leave the ferret's own dishes that cannot be overturned, and a water bottle if none are available in the kennel. Kennels that cooperate this way usually have feeding directions clearly marked on the cage cards. Leave enough of your ferret's own food to last the full time you are gone and about a third extra for spillage.

The floor of a stainless steel dog or cat cage is slippery. Some ferrets will lose control of their hind legs if forced to walk on a slippery floor day after day. If the kennel owner will allow you to do it, leave a piece of carpet (a sample is about the right size) to put on the floor of a cat cage to give the ferret good footing. Some kennels use a piece of corrugated cardboard for the same purpose: this is changed daily to keep the cage cleaner.

Veterinary hospitals sometimes board animals but this is not their main function and ferrets are usually not well housed. The cages are designed for cats or dogs, not for ferrets. The cage doors have widely spaced bars that allow small jills to escape, possibly falling several feet onto a hard floor. The smallest cages are often up near the ceiling, the warmest place in the building. This is ideal for cats, not ferrets, but it is usually where the ferrets are placed because the cage size is appropriate. If this is the type of area where your ferret will have to stay, it is better to make another arrangement. Warm dry air encourages respiratory infections and makes the ferret uncomfortable.

The cardboard disposable cat litter boxes in most kennels are wonderful ferret toys rarely used as intended. Allowing the ferret to have his own litter pan will encourage his usual clean habits.

Ferrets do not like to sleep in an exposed area, especially in unfamiliar surroundings. A sleeping tube or other familiar nest material from home will make them feel more secure.

Bordetella bronchiseptica, a bacterial cause of kennel cough in dogs, may cause respiratory disease in ferrets. Ferrets that will be boarded near dogs should be vaccinated with a killed bacterin. They should have one dose 10 to 14 days before entering the kennel, and a booster the day they arrive. This protects the ferret for about 6 months. If you board your pet again more than 6 months later, he will need a single booster the day he enters the kennel.

FERRET SHOWS

Ferret shows are good sources of information on ferret lore. The animals are beautifully groomed examples of most of the available coat colors. Ferret clubs from around the area are usually represented, and can provide information on anything you need to know about keeping ferrets as pets.

Ferrets are exhibited in cages, and brought to a judging table where the judge examines each animal separately, evaluating its temperament, conformation, coat and color. There are costume classes, yawning contests, and special classes for biggest or smallest ferret, ferret with longest tail, oldest ferret, cutest trick, etc., and classes designed for breeders of special colors and neutered pets.

What is evident in every ferret show is the pleasure people get from their pets, and the tolerant attitude of the ferrets to the fuss made over them. Costume classes display the patience learned by pet ferrets, animals that are not famous for their patience, when buttoned into doll dresses and carried around that way for an hour or more. They rarely

"Ferret Fawcett." Ferrets are not patient animals, but "show ferrets" become very tolerant of this kind of indignity.

try to squirm out of their clothes once they realize you intend them to be subjected to this indignity. They even wear hats with chin straps without trying to scratch them off. Ferrets waiting for judging are seen hanging limply over their owner's arms, passively observing the proceedings.

One danger of ferret shows is that if there is an infectious disease in any of the animals at the show, all those exposed are likely to get sick soon after they go home. Occasionally these are fatal illnesses, although more often they are upper respiratory viruses that cause sneezing for a few days. The problem with infectious diseases is that when everyone goes home with the ferrets that attended the show, all their other ferrets are exposed and hundreds of ferrets not even at the show might also get sick.

Ferrets must have proof of up-to-date boosters for distemper before entering a show, but there are other diseases that cannot be controlled with vaccines. Ferret clubs are run by responsible people who cancel shows rather than expose ferrets to a dangerous infection, but some people are more willing than others to take risks. Electronic mail messages about ferrets alert all interested listeners when there is an outbreak of some sort of illness after a show, and can get the warning to people planning on attending another show in the same area.

FOR MORE INFORMATION ON . . .

Bordetella bronchiseptica, see chapter 14

areas where ferrets are illegal, see Appendix B

chapter 11

REPRODUCTION AND GROWTH OF FERRETS

REPRODUCTION

Spayed jills and neutered hobs make the best pets. The information in this chapter is intended to make you aware of the complexities of breeding ferrets and raising kits, not to encourage you to do it. Birthing problems are common in jills, and can cause the death of your pet if you don't recognize the problem early enough. Some first-time mothers reject or cannibalize their kits. Mastitis (inflammation of the mammary glands) can reduce milk production so much that the kits starve to death in a few days. Baby ferrets grow quickly under ideal conditions, and they die quickly when something goes wrong. Unless you have a lot of time to devote to learning about ferret

Getting a litter of kits to 3 weeks of age may be a time-consuming and energy-draining experience.

reproduction from an experienced person, and to monitoring and caring for the jills and kits, leave ferret breeding to experts.

If the photoperiod (hours of light per day) is correct, jills will be sexually mature at 4 months, and hobs at 6 to 8 months. The natural reproductive cycle of ferrets starts as the hours of daylight gradually lengthen, soon after the New Year.

Jills are "seasonally polyestrous": they have multiple heat cycles but only in the spring and summer. Males come into breeding condition a little earlier in the spring than jills. In the fall and early winter, their testicles are small and may be hard to find, moving away from the scrotum to the inguinal area (the groin). During the breeding season, both males and females have much stronger body odor and greasier skin than usual.

A swollen vulva shows that this jill is in heat. She must be bred, treated with hormones, or spayed in less than a month to avoid severe health problems.

Jills are induced ovulators, that is, they do not ovulate unless breeding takes place. This has serious consequences for the unbred jill. When she is in heat, the jill's vulva swells very noticeably, and there is a pale pink watery secretion. This constant dampness plus the open vulva allows bacteria to reach the opening to the bladder, and some jills develop bladder infections and occasionally bladder stones.

There is very little risk in spaying a jill when she is in heat, if the surgery is done soon after the vulva swelling is noticed. Surgery becomes risky when the jill has been in heat for more than three weeks. In some jills, the estrogen produced during the heat period prevents bone marrow cells from dividing as they generally do, and red cells, white cells and platelets are reduced in numbers. White blood cells provide protection against infection and platelets are required for blood to clot. About 50% of jills that have been in heat a long time gradually become very anemic and weak. They are more susceptible to infection than usual. Very slight injuries cause bleeding because their platelet counts are so low, and some bleed to death through their intestinal tract. Most severely affected jills die even with treatment. Multiple blood transfusions are necessary to save their lives, and although surgery is hazardous, they must be spayed right away to shut off the production of estrogen.

Ferret breeders have the option of controlling a jill's estrus periods by manipulating light cycles, breeding her whenever she comes in heat, or artificially ending an estrus with injectable hormones. Jills come in heat about 6 weeks after a dramatic change in light cycles, for instance going from 8 to 14 hours of light a day. If the light is not bright enough, results will be less predictable. Reducing photoperiod to 8 hours of light prevents most jills from coming in heat.

Injectable hormones given 10 days or more after the swollen vulva is first noticed induce ovulation and end estrus in about a week. They will not work earlier. About 5 days after the injection, there will be a noticeable reduction in vulva swelling. The timing of the next heat is unpredictable, depending on many factors including photoperiod, diet, and the duration of the jill's heat before hormones were used.

For best conception rate and litter size, breed the jill two consecutive days the second week she is in heat. The gestation period is 42 days. An experienced veterinarian or ferret owner can diagnose pregnancy about two weeks after breeding, by feeling for the developing kits in the jill's abdomen.

A jill will return to heat within 2 weeks of weaning a litter if the photoperiod is right. Some jills with small litters will come in heat while still nursing the kits. Under natural light conditions, jills can have two litters a year. If kept under artificial light 14 or more hours a day, they can have three litters a year. If bred on every heat, they will have smaller and smaller litters each time, eventually failing to conceive and giving themselves a rest between litters.

Gestation lasts 6 weeks. This jill has 10 days to go.

KITS FROM BIRTH TO SEXUAL MATURITY

Jills have litters of 1 to 15 kits or more, with an average of 10 in the first litter of a well-nourished jill. Kits weigh only 8 to 10 grams at birth (28 grams = 1 oz), and will fit into a teaspoon, but they triple their weight in 10 days if their mother has a plentiful milk supply. They make a cheeping sound for attention and are helpless for about three weeks. Their skin has a very pungent, bitter odor, probably to discourage predators.

Kits are born with very fine white hair, and within days are quite furry, with a longer mane on the backs of their necks. Those that will be albinos or black-eyed whites remain white, while all other colors turn gray at 5 or 6 days of age. White markings can be distinguished but it is impossible to tell what color the kit will be until it is over three weeks old. Their eyes and ear canals are closed for more than 4 weeks, but they have their first teeth when only two weeks old. Well-nourished, healthy kits sleep or nurse most of the time for their first three weeks.

At three weeks of age kits will weigh about 100 grams, and start to eat solid food, but they still depend on milk for survival. Jills peak in their lactation at this time, and begin to look very lean if they have a large litter. The natural weaning age is 5 to 6 weeks. At six weeks, the difference between male and female kits is noticeable. Female kits weigh 200 to 250 grams, and males over 300 grams. Until they are about 8 weeks old, kits make a sound something like a goose honking when they want attention. The females reach their full size (600 to 800 grams) by 16 weeks of age, but males continue to grow and gain weight until they are 9 or 10 months old.

Newborn kits are completely helpless. They weigh 8 to 10 grams (1/3 ounce) at birth, and will fit into a teaspoon.

CONGENITAL PROBLEMS AND GENETIC DEFECTS

Congenital problems are not necessarily inherited defects. They are structural abnormalities that occur before birth, sometimes caused by viruses or drugs used in the pregnant female. If a female has more than one litter with the same type of defect, and other females that received the same care and treatments during pregnancy did not have similarly affected offspring, the defect is probably inherited.

Some common congenital defects are present at birth and cause death of the newborns. For instance, kits born with their eyes open have other head abnormalities that prevent them from surviving. Occasionally they have no brain.

Because fetal maturation is responsible for initiating labor in the jill, head defects in the unborn kits are often associated with failure of the jill to deliver the litter. The whole litter will die a few days after the due date, and the jill will die also unless the dead kits are removed by cesarean section. Some congenital defects interfere with normal birth, such as necks bent almost double that cannot be straightened. Cesarean delivery is necessary to save the jill's life. Most of the time, we have no idea what induces such abnormalities in the kits, but it is not a big problem and rarely recurs in other litters of the same jill.

Extra toes may be small and barely noticable.

Large extra toes are much more obvious, but cause the ferret no inconvenience.

There are some inherited defects that are harmless, for instance, polydactyly, which means having extra toes. The albino color phase is a defect inherited in ferrets as it is in other animals such as rats and rabbits. Albinism is associated with many minor tissue abnormalities that rarely cause problems in animals.

Other inherited defects can cause various degrees of disability.

CYSTIC KIDNEYS Cystic kidneys have big bubbles of fluid that gradually enlarge and destroy the normal kidney structure. These can be felt from the outside of the ferret, and in a lean ferret, are visible when the animal is held up and stretched out. Often only one kidney is affected and when it is removed the ferret can live a normal life, because only one kidney is necessary for survival. If both kidneys are affected the ferret will die when there is not enough normal tissue left to maintain adequate function. Ferrets are often 2 or 3 years old when these problems are diagnosed, but occasionally cystic kidneys are found in kits soon after weaning.

BRACHYCEPHALY There are strains of ferrets that have short noses like bulldogs: this is called brachycephaly and the animals are called "pugs." If there is not enough room in the short jaw for the ferret's teeth they come in very crooked. Although some people like the pug appearance, it is not a desirable characteristic because of the dental abnormalities that go with it. Breeding ferrets with blunter noses than usual will eventually produce pug ferrets.

CATARACTS Some ferrets have cataracts at a very young age, not associated with any eye injury. This is inherited and these animals are blind. Blind ferrets adapt well to a familiar area and live otherwise normal lives. To avoid producing more blind ferrets, jills or hobs that produce kits with cataracts should be spayed or neutered. A cataract in one eye that appears in a much older animal might be due to an injury rather than being inherited.

This is a normal eye.

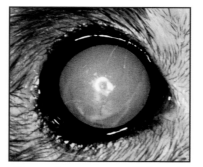

The pearly appearance of this eye is caused by a cataract. Cataracts this severe cause total blindness.

chapter 12

FERRET NUTRITION

IMPORTANCE OF A GOOD DIET

Nutrition is the most important single factor in keeping ferrets healthy. If a poor diet is selected early in the pet's life, it becomes difficult to force the ferret to change to a different flavor. The inferior food will cause health problems that vary from poor coat to bladder stones. Young ferrets fed an inadequate diet will be stunted and will have dry, sparse, lusterless coats. Jills will fail to conceive or have small litters. Newborns will die if the mother is not fed properly during pregnancy and lactation. Pets fed poor quality protein are more susceptible to infections and parasites. Bladder stones can cause complete bladder obstruction. This is life threatening and requires immediate veterinary attention.

The five groups of nutrients that all animals require are proteins, fats, carbohydrates, vitamins and minerals. Fatty acids are the structural units of fats and amino acids are the structural units of proteins. Ferrets require a fatty acid (arachidonic acid) and two amino acids (arginine and taurine) that are not found in sufficient quantities in any plant material. A ferret is therefore an obligate carnivore. You cannot feed it a vegetarian diet without endangering its life.

Ferrets have a very short, simple intestinal tract. The large intestine and cecum of most animals contain bacteria that digest the complex carbohydrates found in vegetables and grains. Ferrets have an especially short large intestine and no cecum, and therefore cannot digest any but the simplest carbohydrates, such as starch and sugars.

It takes only 3 hours for a morsel of food to be swallowed by a ferret, pass through the digestive tract and come out in the litter box. This rapid passage time means that digestion of food is inefficient compared to other animals. Some food is passed unchanged from one end of the intestine to another because it is not exposed to the digestive enzymes and the lining of the gut for long enough to be completely absorbed. If you want to see how little a ferret's intestine changes the food he eats, feed him dark colored pellets in the morning, then take them away and feed light colored pellets. If you check the litter box in the evening, there will be two different colors of stool, and sometimes the same piece of stool will be divided into light and dark areas.

A good diet for a ferret has to be:
- high in energy (calories)
- high in protein
- low in fiber

WHAT YOU CAN LEARN FROM THE LABEL ON A BAG OF FOOD

1. Is the food intended for a particular category or age of animal?

Good quality pet foods have been tested on animals to make sure the diet is adequate. If a food is meant for a particular stage of life, for instance growth of young animals, or if it is adequate for all stages of life, the bag label will say so. The initials AAFCO (Association of American Feed Control Officials) will appear with the statement.

2. What are the ingredients in the food?

The ingredients of commercial animal diets must be listed on the container label, but the quantities of each ingredient are not specified. However, the ingredients are listed in order according to the amount of each in the food. For instance, grocery store cat foods list ground yellow corn as the first and therefore major ingredient. Ferret diets should list meat, fish or poultry meal or by-products as the first ingredient. Look for a label that also lists other animal products, such as liver meal, eggs, or blood meal, when selecting a ferret diet. Sometimes manufacturers list several different kinds of grain right after meat or poultry meal. The total amount of grain might exceed the amount of poultry meal in the diet.

Typical ingredients in a good ferret diet, as listed on the label:

Chicken by-products, herring meal, corn, cod fish, animal liver, dried beet pulp, brewers dried yeast, cane molasses, salt, sodium propionate, DL-methionine, L-lysine, taurine, vitamin A, vitamin D3 supplement, vitamin E supplement, riboflavin supplement, niacin, biotin, choline chloride, folic acid, thiamine mononitrate, pyridoxine hydrochloride, BHA, vitamin B12 supplement, menadione sodium bisulfite complex (a source of vitamin K), D calcium pantothenate, manganese oxide, inositol, ascorbic acid, iron sulfate, copper sulfate, zinc oxide, cobalt carbonate, potassium iodide, sodium selenite.

3. What nutrients are in the food?

The **guaranteed analysis** lists the percentages of crude protein, crude fat, fiber, ash and moisture.

Crude protein is the total amount of protein in the food, but it says nothing about its digestibility. The quality of the protein is very important. Tendons and plant seeds contain protein, but ferrets cannot digest them. Compare the analysis to the ingredients list. If most of the protein is from poultry or meat meal, about 80% of it will be digestible. Protein from meat by-products, which contain variable amounts of hooves and tendons and hair, or from ground yellow corn, is much less digestible. The label on some premium quality foods will tell you the digestibility of the protein. Good quality protein is expensive. The lower the price of the food, the more likely it is that the crude protein is of poor quality and low digestibility. Ferret diets should contain over 30% crude protein, of high digestibility.

Crude fat includes all the fat in the diet, from both plant and animal sources. Not all types of fat are equally digestible. Ferrets need animal source fats, and prefer the flavor of animal fats. Some generic cat foods are very palatable to ferrets because they are sprayed with animal fat after the pellet is formed. Generic cat foods contain 8 to 10% fat, not nearly enough for a ferret diet, which should contain at least 15% fat. If a generic cat food is the ferret's only source of fat, he will have a poor coat and dry, itchy skin. Diets containing 30 to 40% fat are suitable for growing and lactating ferrets, but pets will become obese on palatable high fat foods. If extra fat is added to an otherwise poor quality diet, the ferret will eat enough to get the calories he needs, but may not get sufficient protein to maintain his body condition and health. Complete ferret diets and premium cat foods contain the correct balance of good quality animal fat and protein for your pet.

Fiber is undigestible carbohydrate that adds bulk to the diet. Fiber causes an increase in the quantity of stool, and interferes with digestion of other nutrients, which is why animal foods intended for weight reduction contain high levels of fiber. Sources of fiber include plant hulls, such as oat bran, or vegetable material such as beet pulp. There should be 4% or less fiber in foods intended for ferrets.

Ash is the mineral left if the food is completely burned. It is an indicator of the level of mineral available to the animal that eats the food. It should be less than 7% in a ferret diet. Excessive ash in the diet was once believed to be the most important factor in the production of bladder stones, but it is now known that there are several factors involved, and ash is not the most important.

Most dry cat foods contain about 10% moisture and 90% dry matter. The dry matter contains all of the protein, fat and other nutrients. There are usually over 1800 calories per pound of premium quality cat food. An adult pet ferret requires about 200 calories per pound of body weight daily.

Canned cat food can be of very good quality and is usually more digestible than dry food, but ferrets have a very small capacity intestine. Over 70% of canned food is water. Ferrets can't eat enough canned cat food to take in the calories they need. This is especially true for pregnant jills, when a lot of the space in the abdomen is occupied by the kits and there is little room left for bulky food. Canned foods may tempt a ferret to eat when it has been sick, or can supplement the regular diet. Eating an entirely soft diet causes rapid build-up of plaque on a ferret's teeth.

Typical guaranteed analysis for a good ferret diet:

    Crude protein 38.0%
    Crude fat 18.0%
    Fiber 3.5%
    Ash 6.5%
    Moisture 10.0%

SPECIAL FEEDING REQUIREMENTS
Pregnancy, growth and lactation

Jills often have 10 or more kits in their first litter, and must be fed very well during their pregnancy to be able to deliver the kits and nurse them. To conceive this many kits in a litter, the first-time jill must be well grown and receive high quality protein. Breeding ferrets require more protein in their diet than spayed and neutered pets, and growing kits and lactating jills require a high fat diet with excellent quality protein.

Kits are weaned naturally when they are about 6 weeks old. Until then, they get most of their nutrition from their mother's milk, which is very rich in both protein and fat. Cows' milk is about 4% fat, while ferret milk, 3 weeks after birth of the kits, is about 20% fat. This allows the kits to grow very quickly, but it also drains from the jill energy that must be replaced by feeding her a very high quality diet. Nursing jills must eat two or three times as much as usual to nourish both themselves and the kits. If they have big litters of more than 10 kits, they will lose weight no matter what you feed them. They can't take in as much energy as they are expending in making milk for the kits.

To relieve the jills as much as possible, offer the babies moist food when they will begin to try it, at 3 weeks of age. Supplementing a nursing jill's pelleted diet with a moist diet once or twice a day increases her food and fluid intake and stimulates milk production. Healthy, robust kits have been raised on both ferret diets and premium cat foods. The pelleted food is soaked in warm water to make a porridge, and offered to the litter on a flat tray 2 to 4 times a day, depending on your schedule. Extra fat or cooked egg can be added to increase its nutritional value, but be careful not to unbalance the original diet. Remove food uneaten after an hour. If it is left with the litter, the kits will crawl through it. They will learn to use this wet area for a toilet, interfering with litter training and possibly spreading parasites. The jill will not eat contaminated food if she has any choice.

Nursing jills need two or three times more water than usual, and they will drink much more from a dish than a water bottle. If they don't drink enough, they will not eat enough and their milk supply will go down.

Three-week-old kits can be fed cows' milk and whipping cream, mixed half and half, to supplement (but not replace) their mother's milk if she can't quite manage to keep up with the demands of a large litter. Kits don't learn to drink well from a dish until they are about four weeks old, so they must be hand fed until then. Plastic droppers are best for feeding them by hand. If hand feeding is their only source of nutrition, use kitten or puppy milk replacers for ferret kits. They need frequent feeding (at two or three hour intervals) when two to three weeks old, and after that can get by on four meals a day. They prefer warm milk, especially when very young.

Pets with urinary tract infections and bladder stones

Ferrets fed generic cat foods containing mainly plant protein are particularly susceptible to bladder stones. Digestion of protein produces chemical compounds that must be excreted in the urine. The products formed from the digestion of plant proteins make the urine alkaline.
Magnesium salts form struvite crystals in alkaline urine, and stones form as crystals accumulate and stick together. These cause complete obstruction and death in untreated male ferrets, and chronic problems with partial obstruction in females. Eating meat protein makes the urine more acidic, and reduces the likelihood of bladder stones forming. Urinary tract infections increase susceptibility to stones. Ferrets with bladder infections should be fed the best quality meat protein possible.

Bladder stones may be very large single stones (top left), "sand" which can cause complete obstruction of the bladder (top right), or multiple small to large stones (bottom right).

Respiratory infections

Ferrets with upper respiratory infections (colds) cannot breathe well through their noses and often eat poorly. They can't smell the food and it's hard to swallow with blocked nostrils. First clean the ferret's nose so that he can breathe. Then add water to his favorite pellets, microwave for 10-15 seconds to soften the food, stir it well, and give it to the ferret warm. Heating makes the odor stronger and the softer texture is often accepted by sick ferrets.

Insulinomas

Ferrets with insulin-producing tumors have low blood sugar most of the time. To keep blood sugar as stable as possible, the ferret should eat high protein foods frequently. Most ferrets do this anyway, but to make sure he does, offer him a little Nutrical or other small animal nutritional supplement he likes, or a small volume of a human nutritional supplement, such as Ensure Plus, several times a day.

Ferrets with insulin problems should not be fed high sugar snacks, unless their blood glucose has gone so low that they must have sugar to bring them out of a hypoglycemic attack. The sugar, usually given as corn syrup, can be followed by Nutrical or Ensure as a source of protein and fat.

Anorexia due to illness

Sick ferrets need special attention. They often have a reduced appetite when they need good food. The secret to feeding a sick animal is to offer it a small amount of a palatable, nutritious food frequently. The patient will often take a few bites of anything you offer, then will not return to that food again. However, every time you bring food, he will taste it. He will eat a much larger quantity of food if you offer many small meals rather than one large one. When the ferret has lost interest in the special food, remove it, so that it will not get sour or stale and cause him to reject the same food next time you bring it.

Jills need about 200 calories and males over 300 calories a day to maintain their body weight. Chronically ill ferrets have been maintained on nothing but Nutrical, Ensure Plus or other easily digested nutritional supplements for months at a time. Some sick ferrets will eat their own pelleted diet only if one of these supplements is mixed with it.

chapter 13

PARASITES

INTESTINAL PARASITES

Intestinal worms are rarely a problem in ferrets. A baby ferret should have at least one stool sample checked for parasites when he is first adopted. The same test will identify several different parasites that shed eggs into the animal's stool. Roundworms are common in puppies and kittens but rare in ferrets, therefore ferrets need not be automatically treated for roundworms as other pets are.

Ferrets may be infected by three species of intestinal parasites in a biological group known as protozoans. Two species, *Giardia lamblia* and *Cryptosporidium parvum*, are potentially communicable to man. The third, a species of coccidia, is communicable to other carnivores, including but not necessarily limited to other mustelids, dogs and cats.

Giardiasis is uncommon in ferrets but has been known to occur in those that drink contaminated water or eat contaminated feed, especially uncooked offal. Although the cysts (the equivalent of eggs) may be found in the ferret's stool, the animal rarely shows any clinical signs related to the parasite. Humans suffer mild to severe diarrhea and abdominal pain when infected with giardia, and there is a possibility that people could be infected by ferrets carrying this disease. However, this has never been reported, and giardiasis is uncommon in pet ferrets kept inside and fed pelleted diets and clean water. Baby ferrets may acquire the infection from puppies or kittens in the same pet shop. The treatment for giardiasis is the same for animals as for people, and must be prescribed by a veterinarian.

Cryptosporidiosis is common in young ferrets fed uncooked offal. This parasite may be acquired from cattle that often carry it. Human beings with cryptosporidiosis have mild to severe watery diarrhea and a flu-like syndrome. Although baby ferrets might infect people, this has never been reported. Ferrets do not usually have diarrhea associated with this infection. There is no effective treatment for cryptosporidiosis, but the person's or animal's immune system eventually eliminates the parasite. People who have AIDS or other immunodeficiency, or those on immunosuppressive drugs for allergies, arthritis or cancer, should not handle baby ferrets. Even a kit that has never had raw beef products could get cryptosporidiosis from its mother.

Coccidiosis is common in ferrets and sometimes causes bloody diarrhea in juvenile pets. There are many species of coccidia and usually each species infects a limited range of similar animals. For instance, coccidia of sheep and goats do not infect dogs, cats or ferrets. Ferret coccidia will also infect dogs, cats and probably similar animals like foxes or wolves, but not other types of animals such as cattle or sheep. Ferrets may get coccidiosis at the breeding farm of origin or while in a pet shop when exposed to infected puppies or kittens. Adult animals rarely have coccidiosis because they become immune to it when young. People are resistant to coccidiosis.

A debilitated, dehydrated ferret with diarrhea due to coccidiosis may require hospitalization for a day to be rehydrated with injections of electrolytes. Replacing a poor quality diet with one or more ferret diets or premium cat foods helps sick kits recover more quickly.

Most of the time, even when a fecal sample is positive for coccidia oocysts (eggs), it causes no obvious problem to the ferret. To improve the pet's general health and prevent transmission of coccidiosis to other pets, the kit should be treated with one of several drugs available. Treatment must be given for 10 consecutive days for any drug to eliminate coccidia from the gastrointestinal tract. A fecal sample should be checked about a week after the last dose to make sure the treatment was effective. The oocysts shed in the stool do not become infectious for at least one day. Cleaning the litter box thoroughly each day helps to control the parasite and prevent re-infestation.

HEARTWORM DISEASE

The most dangerous parasite for ferrets is the heartworm (*Dirofilaria immitis*) that infects dogs and sometimes cats. Heartworms mature in the chambers of the heart and block major arteries, causing heart failure and death. Because ferret hearts are so small, it takes only a few worms to kill a ferret.

A ferret with heartworms will seem tired all the time, may have a chronic cough, and becomes very short of breath if it is active for even a few minutes. Fluid builds up in the abdomen because of the failing heart and blocked blood vessels. The disease is rapidly progressive and fatal. Cardiomyopathy, another heart condition of ferrets, can cause identical symptoms.

There is a blood test to diagnose adult heartworms in dogs. It is not 100% accurate in ferrets because it is affected by the number of worms in the animal's body. The more worms there are, the more likely the test is to identify them. This test is used to differentiate cardiomyopathy from heartworm disease, but it might not be sensitive enough to identify the presence of just one worm, which is enough to cause a heart problem in a small ferret.

HEARTWORM PREVENTION

A microfilaria is an intermediate stage of the life cycle of the heartworm. Adult heartworms live and breed in the host's heart, and release microfilariae into the blood stream where they can be picked up by a biting mosquito. If a mosquito bites an infected dog or ferret, it cannot infect a susceptible animal bitten the same day. It takes at least 10 days for microfilariae to develop to an infectious stage in the mouthparts of the insect.

Drugs are used in dogs, and can be used in ferrets, to kill the infectious microfilariae transmitted to them by mosquito bites, preventing mature heartworms from developing. These drugs do not kill adult heartworms. A different drug can be used to kill adult heartworms, but the treatment is risky in dogs because the dead worms block arteries. There is even more risk with ferrets because of their smaller blood vessels. It is much safer to prevent heartworms developing.

Ferrets that either live outside or spend a significant amount of time outside or in an unscreened house are at risk of heartworm infection. Preventive drugs can be given once daily or once monthly depending on the specific drug selected. Medication must be given for the whole time mosquitoes are active, which will vary with geographical location. In tropical areas, susceptible pets should be on heartworm prevention year-round.

Dogs are tested to make sure they don't already have heartworms before starting the medication, which could have bad side effects if adult heartworms are present in the heart or arteries. Your veterinarian will probably do a blood test to make sure your ferret is not already infected, before starting it on heartworm prevention.

Alternatively, ferrets can be housed indoors in well-screened rooms and never taken outside to play, a wise choice for several other reasons.

EXTERNAL PARASITES
Ear mites

Probably most ferrets have ear mites (*Otodectes cynotes*) at some time in their lives. They can be acquired from or spread to dogs, cats, and other ferrets. If you own both a cat and ferret, and one of them has ear mites, the other probably does too, unless there is no contact at all between the two animals. Ear mites don't live long off the host, and are unlikely to be carried from place to place by a human being, the way fleas often are. However, cats and ferrets that sleep in the same areas, even at different times of the day, can transmit ear mites to each another. It takes about three weeks for the parasite to go through its whole life cycle, from egg to mature mite.

Mite eggs are resistant to treatment. Treatments should be carried out keeping this in mind. One treatment kills only the mature mites. After a few days, if no further treatment is given, a new generation will have hatched from eggs in and around the ear. Medication used in the ear is effective for only a few days, and a single treatment will rarely kill 100% of the mature mites. It therefore takes at least two treatments, and usually more, spaced at one to three week intervals, to truly eliminate ear mites. Shortening the treatment intervals will kill the adults faster and reduce the symptoms of infestation. It will make no difference to the length of time treatment is needed, because this depends on the rate at which mite eggs hatch.

Any ear medication safe to use in cats is safe for ferrets. If the ears are inflamed, it is best to use a medication to control infection and inflammation before using any anti-mite treatment. A veterinarian can prescribe a suitable otic ointment. When infection is controlled, use the anti-mite treatment as directed by your veterinarian. Depending on the type of medication, this is often once a week for a few weeks, then about once a month to completely control mites. Spray the ferret with a flea killer to destroy any mites on the coat. The tip of the tail is a spot that mites may be hiding, because the ferret sleeps with his tail tip near his ears. When persistent treatment eventually rids a pet of ear mites, his ears will rarely need cleaning.

FLEAS

Another external parasite that affects ferrets is the dog or cat flea. Ferrets can be seriously debilitated by a heavy flea burden. Fleas bite and suck blood from the wounds they make, causing anemia. They cause itchy skin and sometimes allergies that make the hair fall out. The most common place to find fleas on a ferret is between the shoulder blades.

Most of the fleas are in the house, not on the animals. Any flea control program has to kill not only fleas on all pets that spend any time in the house, but also everywhere the animals can go. The most intense effort should be concentrated on the areas where the ferrets, cats or dogs sleep. Eggs will hatch into larvae in these areas. Larvae eat the droppings of mature fleas and become pupae, which live in cocoons and eventually emerge as a new generation of mature fleas.

Because fleas can cause serious health problems, every effort should be made to eliminate them. Using cedar litter seems to keep fleas out of the ferret's cage without using other types of chemical control. Cedar litter is not toxic for ferrets and no allergic reactions have been reported.

If fleas are discovered on your ferret, several steps will have to be taken to eliminate them:

Remove all fabric bedding from the ferret's cage or nest and wash it. Adult fleas will not stay long on a bare metal surface, but eggs, larvae and pupae will, so the cage should be washed and sprayed with flea killer and vacuumed weekly. The litter box in the cage should be emptied and cleaned as usual.

Fleas cannot jump higher than 24". If you have a severe flea problem in the house because of other pets, raise the ferret's cage off the floor. Don't allow the ferret out of the cage in an infested area, and prevent other pets from climbing onto the cage.

Bathe the ferret with a flea shampoo or with a regular shampoo followed by a flea dip safe for cats.

Treat all other susceptible animals in the house.

Vacuum the house thoroughly, paying special attention to areas where any of the pets habitually lie down: this is where the flea eggs and other stages of the life cycle will be concentrated.

There are sprays, bombs and granules on the market that kill the eggs and larval stages of the parasites' life cycle for several months. However, the pupal stage, which hatches a new flea, is very difficult to kill.

Some fleas will evade the first treatment, and new fleas constantly emerge from pupae. The ferret must be shampooed, sprayed, or dipped weekly for a few consecutive weeks to prevent reinfestation. This is not harmful when the products are used as directed on the label. Any spray, dip or shampoo safe for cats is safe for ferrets, even for nursing kits. Ferrets don't like to be sprayed and must be held firmly or scruffed to get a thorough treatment.

chapter 14

RESPIRATORY INFECTIONS

Upper respiratory infections are common in both young and mature ferrets. Some human cold viruses are infectious for ferrets, as is human influenza. Early research on human influenza used ferrets as models of the disease.

Baby ferrets are more susceptible to respiratory disease when they are stressed by a combination of weaning, overcrowding, and poor housing. They may be exposed to influenza and cold viruses when sold to pet shops, taken to shows, or taken home by new owners. At pet shops, the ventilation and room temperature might not be ideal. Other animals at the same shop might need a warmer environment than the ferrets. Unless there are separate rooms with individual ventilation and heating systems, which some major pet shops have, the ferrets are too warm. Many kits are shipped by air, exposing them, and humans who travel by plane, to a great variety of respiratory viruses.

Ferrets that go to shows are exposed to human and ferret viruses while subjected to extra stress, and less than ideal ventilation, depending on what type of building is housing the show.

Most ferrets with respiratory diseases are no sicker than a human child with a cold. A ferret with flu or a cold will be noticed sneezing, and if you look closely, you will see a slight nasal discharge, like a wet moustache near the nostrils. Sneezing and runny noses are rarely caused by allergies in ferrets, although some are irritated by dusty clay litter. Either influenza or cold viruses usually cause a less severe disease in ferrets than in people. However, bacterial infections may be superimposed on the original disease in stressed animals, and these may require veterinary treatment.

Most ferrets, like most people, will be much better in a couple of days. If not, the ferret should be taken to a veterinarian, who may prescribe antibiotics. It is difficult to give pills to ferrets, but they cooperate very well when treated with sweet-flavored pediatric antibiotic suspensions. They usually need treatment for 5 to 7 days.

Ferrets boarded at veterinary hospitals or at animal boarding facilities may be infected with *Bordetella bronchiseptica*, one cause of kennel cough in dogs. This bacterial disease can make stressed ferrets very sick, causing a thick yellowish nasal discharge that blocks the nostrils. If untreated, some develop pneumonia that responds poorly to antibiotics. Occasionally, the bacteria produce a toxin that causes convulsions and coma.

The best way to avoid *Bordetella bronchiseptica* infection is either not to board the ferret where there are dogs, or have it vaccinated before it enters the kennel. There is a killed *Bordetella* bacterin intended for dogs that works well in ferrets. It must be given at least 10 days before exposure to infection to have its greatest effect, and the ferret should have a booster the day he enters the kennel. There is also an intranasal vaccine for dogs that contains live bacteria and canine parainfluenza virus. This vaccine may induce disease in ferrets and is not recommended for them.

Some boarding kennels house ferrets in the same area as cats, which less frequently carry *Bordetella*. It is still wise to have the ferret vaccinated when boarded, because the bacteria are airborne and can be carried on hands.

NUTRITIONAL DIARRHEA

Mild diarrhea is common in ferrets because they have a short, inefficient intestinal tract that is very sensitive to changes in diet. Ferrets often eat non-nutritive substances, such as wood shavings used for bedding and pieces of cloth or rubber. If they manage to pass the foreign body through their intestine, they often pass green mucus with it. Green mucus is not characteristic of any particular disease in a ferret, it just shows that something has irritated his gut lining.

Dairy products invariably cause loose stool in ferrets. Most ferrets love milk and will take medication, such as heartworm prevention tablets, in a small amount of milk. Nutritional diarrhea stops when the food that caused it is eliminated from the diet. It is not harmful to the ferret but it may distress you, particularly if the ferret has an accident on a rug. This type of diarrhea usually lasts only a short time, and rarely causes dehydration if the ferret is at liberty to drink all the water he wants. If a ferret is given a food that causes diarrhea for several days consecutively, dehydration might result, and the stress might induce a secondary infectious diarrheal disease.

INFECTIOUS DIARRHEA

Diarrhea can be caused by infections with:

   A) parasites
   B) bacteria
   C) viruses

A) **Coccidiosis** is the only parasitic disease that commonly causes diarrhea in ferrets. It is more common for coccidia eggs (called oocysts) to be found in stool samples from apparently normal, healthy ferrets. Diarrhea occasionally occurs in recently weaned kits stressed by other things such as overcrowding in a pet shop, travelling, or poor nutrition. The stool is often bloody and the kit might strain, moan and prolapse rectal tissue when defecating. Newly purchased kits should be examined by a veterinarian soon after purchase, and have a stool sample checked for parasites.

B) There are two bacterial diseases, proliferative colitis and *Helicobacter mustelae* gastritis, that can affect any age ferret, but most commonly cause diarrhea and severe weight loss in 12 to 20-week-old animals.

Proliferative colitis is caused by bacteria that are not contagious to other kinds of animals. The tissue lining the large intestine or the last part of the small intestine becomes very thick, interfering with absorption of nutrients and water. Ferrets with this infection have dark stool, often containing a large amount of clear or green mucus. If not treated properly, these ferrets will lose half their body weight in a week. They strain and moan or cry in pain while defecating. Sometimes rectal tissue is prolapsed and may not return to its normal position for hours or days. These animals will continue to eat with a reduced appetite, but are inactive and lethargic. They will eventually die if not given the appropriate medication.

There is no laboratory test available to confirm the diagnosis, however, the thickened area of affected intestine can sometimes be felt from the outside of the ferret and can be seen on x-rays. The treatment for proliferative colitis usually brings about a quick recovery.

Helicobacter mustelae gastritis affects ferrets at the same age as proliferative colitis, and causes similar symptoms. This bacterial organism is related to the one associated with gastritis and ulcers in human beings, and the treatment for ferrets is the same one used in people. Ferrets with ulcers have very dark, tarry-looking stool. Gastritis causes abdominal pain and most of these animals don't eat well or at all. They lose weight very quickly and will die without appropriate treatment. Often animals that have ulcers develop colitis, and vice versa.

Many healthy-looking ferrets carry the organisms that cause these two diseases. Stress reduces the animal's resistance and induces diarrhea and wasting. Minimize stress to a young growing ferret to avoid these and other health problems.

The common stresses associated with colitis and ulcers are environmental, most often poor diet or inadequate feeding. Ferrets that accidentally are fasted for a day or more are most susceptible. This might happen if someone forgets to fill the water bottle, or if the ferret is prevented somehow from eating or drinking for a day. Ferrets that can't get water will not eat dry food, therefore water deprivation immediately leads to food deprivation.

Overcrowding or keeping the ferret in an excessively warm environment is also very stressful. Ferrets are most comfortable at temperatures below 70°F. Although they like to sleep in a pile, they need a reasonable amount of space for eating, drinking, and playing. There is no strict rule about what this space might be. If a litter box or toilet area can be kept clean by once a day cleaning, the number of animals using it is not excessive. If the litter box is always dirty, there are probably too many animals in that area.

If your ferret begins to have chronic diarrhea, and loses weight, take it to a veterinarian as soon as possible. Ulcers cause blood loss and weight loss. These animals will die in a few days when a large bleeding ulcer has developed, and the chances that the healing drugs will have time to save the animal's life grow slimmer as time passes.

TREATMENT OF WASTING DISEASES. It is impossible to be absolutely sure that any wasted ferret does not have both proliferative colitis and gastritis/ulcers at once, and the best treatment is therefore a combination of the drug regimes for the two diseases. Ferrets tolerate these drugs very well. An improvement in appetite and attitude can often be seen within 2 days of beginning treatment. Your veterinarian might take a blood sample to eliminate the possibility that other health problems exist in a wasted ferret, and will check a stool sample for coccidia. Some ferrets are severely dehydrated when first examined and require hospitalization for their initial treatment. After this, the medication can be given at home. Although 10 days is the prescribed period of treatment, some ferrets will suffer a relapse after this and need to go back on antibiotics for a longer time. Do not hesitate to return to your veterinarian if your pet shows any signs of diarrhea or weight loss when the drugs are stopped. The longer you wait to correct the situation, the poorer the ferret's chances are of surviving.

Nutrition plays a large part in allowing the ferret to recover from one of the wasting diseases. Gastritis causes loss of appetite and you might need to administer a high calorie digestible food supplement such as Nutrical to get the ferret over the first few days of treatment, until he starts to feel like eating. He cannot heal unless he eats and must have both protein and calories during this time. Other supplements that ferrets like include the veterinary product Prescription Diet A/D, "Ensure Plus," a product made for human consumption, and several supplements made for human infants. Avoid synthetic milk-based and soy baby formulas which will cause worse diarrhea. Home-made supplements can be concocted. Most ferrets like milk with extra cream and egg yolk added. It will cause diarrhea but enough is absorbed that the ferret will gain weight anyway.

Even healthy animals absorb small meals frequently fed better than one large meal. The first few days of the treatment period for wasted ferrets are critical and even a single mouthful of a nutritious food can make a big difference to the chances of recovery. No amount of time or effort is wasted in tempting sick ferrets to eat frequently.

Ferrets that recover fully from either proliferative colitis or *Helicobacter* gastritis rarely suffer a relapse. The diseases are contagious but are most commonly spread from the mother to her babies, not between adult pets. Isolating a sick ferret from other pets is not necessary to protect the exposed ferrets, although it may be advantageous to give the sick one some privacy. The chances are, if the ferrets have been living together, all of them already have the bacteria in their gastrointestinal tracts, and only those made susceptible by stress will develop the illness.

C) In 1993, a severe, life-threatening diarrhea was reported in ferrets that went to shows on the Atlantic coast, or were exposed to ferrets that went to the shows. Because of the character of the diarrhea, this disease became known as "green slime disease." Previously healthy animals developed diarrhea when exposed to apparently normal ferrets that had recovered from diarrhea several months earlier, suggesting that the agent, probably a corona virus, is carried for a long time after recovery. This type of diarrhea usually affects mature ferrets, not kits or even juveniles. Affected ferrets have greenish watery diarrhea and become severely dehydrated. Most would die in a few days without adequate treatment, and many die in spite of intensive care because they are unable to digest and absorb food. A ferret that has watery diarrhea for more than 12 hours is at risk of dying of dehydration. Because some of these animals are so sick, home treatment is not appropriate. They must be hospitalized until the acute part of the disease is under control, because they require intravenous feeding and electrolytes.

The lining of the small intestine is responsible for absorbing nutrients. If it is severely damaged by the diarrhea virus, the ferret becomes chronically unable to properly digest food. These ferrets have intermittent bouts of diarrhea, depending partly on their diet. They need a well-balanced, easily digested diet and a constant supply of food. Nutritional supplements might be necessary for months or for the rest of the ferret's life. Some animals have eventually returned to normal, others never can eat normally and die after several months of intense effort by their owner.

The best way to avoid this disease is not to take your ferret to shows, and not to go yourself. The virus can be carried on shoes, hands and clothing. You must be careful where you buy ferrets if you buy from a breeder. Some breeders attend ferret shows, and if their own animals have survived the illness these ferrets will be resistant to the disease but may carry it. If you happen to buy one of these perfectly well ferrets and bring it into a household of susceptible ferrets, you will have an outbreak of diarrhea that can kill as many as half your pets. You will have to decide what risks you are willing to take.

MISCELLANEOUS CAUSES OF DIARRHEA
There are other things that contribute to diarrhea in ferrets, including some kinds of cancer such as lymphosarcoma. Old ferrets with kidney failure often have intermittent diarrhea. Eosinophilic enteritis, possibly caused by an unidentified parasite, causes chronic wasting. A white blood cell count is done to distinguish it from other wasting diseases. There is always a possibility that the ferret has two or more diseases contributing to diarrhea. Several diagnostic tests may be required to sort out the ferret's problems before effective treatment can begin.

VOMITING

The usual cause of vomiting in ferrets is a foreign body in the stomach or upper intestine. The most common foreign bodies are pieces of rubber that they have deliberately eaten, or hairballs from accidentally swallowing masses of hair during their molting period.

Ferrets kept under natural light cycles shed their coats in late fall and spring. Particularly in spring, ferrets shed hair very dramatically. If they live in a home kept lighted until 9 o'clock or later every night, their shedding periods will not be as predictable. They do groom themselves, more or less, depending on the individual, but they also pick up a considerable amount of loose hair from their bedding. Shedding ferrets can be brushed daily to collect as much loose hair as possible, and they can be shampooed once or twice weekly for the same purpose. Their bedding should be changed more frequently than usual, and the cage and play area can be vacuumed. These steps will reduce the chance that ferrets will get hairballs.

Not all ferrets with hairballs will vomit. Some will just stop eating, or eat very little, and pass thin, ribbon-like stools in very small quantities. If the stool is teased apart it will be found to contain a great quantity of hair. The treatment for this is simple and effective most of the time. There are many commercially available, palatable, malt-based laxatives for cats, and a few for ferrets. These come in tubes like toothpaste, and can be fed directly from the tube, or dispensed along the edge of the ferret's dish. Most ferrets will eat any amount offered. To prevent hairballs, each animal should get about an inch of paste per day during its molting period.

To treat a ferret that doesn't appear ill but is vomiting or has suddenly stopped eating or is passing thin stool as described, offer a couple of inches of paste several times the first day. If there is no improvement by the second day a veterinarian should see the ferret, which might have another kind of foreign body or another disease. If the ferret is better the second day, continue the treatment at a reduced dosage. This laxative can cause severe diarrhea if the ferret is allowed to eat all he wants, which might be the whole tube. Four or five inches a day is maximum for home treatment.

Ferrets with other types of foreign bodies might not respond much to the laxative treatment. Some ferrets will chew up cloth, and laxative usually relieves this type of blockage. However, ferrets love to chew any kind of rubber, and this often will cause a complete obstruction that is life-threatening and will not be moved with laxative. These ferrets will get very sick overnight. They might not vomit more than once, but refuse to eat and become dehydrated. They look very ill, with half-closed eyes. A ferret in this state requires immediate veterinary attention. Surgery is necessary to remove rubber or other hard bits of foreign material from the intestine. Most ferrets recover from surgery very well.

chapter 15

TWO VIRAL DISEASES THAT KILL FERRETS

CANINE DISTEMPER
Disease caused by distemper

Ferrets and their close biologic relatives, including the wild black-footed ferret and both wild and domestic mink, are very susceptible to the canine distemper virus. A ferret that begins to show signs of distemper will almost surely die despite any kind of treatment. Ferrets with distemper look very sick right from the start. They have crusted noses, lips, chins and eyes. Their eyes are painful so they keep them closed. They run a high fever and are sleepy and quiet. Their feet often swell and the pads become hard and crusty. The area around the anal opening becomes swollen and red. Some animals will have diarrhea which causes dehydration. The virus eventually infects the brain and causes convulsions.

Prevention of distemper

The only way to avoid the disease is to make sure your pet is vaccinated properly beginning at 9 or 10 weeks of age. Distemper virus is carried and shed in the urine of dogs that have had the disease and recovered, and those that are protected by vaccination but have contacted the virus. Distemper virus may be carried on the shoes of people walking where the carrier dog has urinated. A ferret that never leaves the house can have distemper virus brought to him by his owner. All ferrets should be vaccinated, even if they will never step foot outside.

Jills that are protected by vaccination will pass some of their immunity to their babies in the colostrum, the milk that the kits get the first couple of days of their lives. This passive immunity lasts about 9 weeks, and prevents vaccination being effective in these young animals. Vaccines given during the first 6 or 7 weeks probably give little or no protection. If a series of vaccinations is given at 9, 12 and 14 to 16 weeks, ferrets will be well protected. If the last vaccination is given at 12 weeks, some ferrets with an unusually large amount of passive immunity will not respond strongly enough to vaccination. These ferrets may get distemper if heavily exposed to the virus.

Vaccination for distemper

There is a distemper vaccine made for ferrets. Vaccines made for mink are safe and effective in ferrets, but most distemper vaccines made for dogs are not safe in ferrets and should not be given. Many ferrets have died of distemper after vaccination with dog vaccines. All canine distemper vaccines contain live virus, modified so that is safe for the animal for which it is intended. Ferrets are more susceptible to distemper virus than dogs, and virus modified for dogs is not necessarily modified sufficiently to be safe for ferrets. The first vaccination is particularly important, when the kit has very little immunity left from his mother. Dog vaccines are more likely to cause distemper in this age of ferret than if given as a booster to an adult. It is much safer to let a knowledgeable veterinarian administer the proper vaccine than take a chance on a cheaper and possibly lethal product that you order from a catalog.

RABIES

Ferrets are susceptible to rabies but it is a rare disease in this species compared to dogs and especially cats. Part of the reason for this is an inborn resistance to rabies. The occurrence of rabies in closely related wild animals such as weasels and mink is very low. Ferrets have very thick, tough skin and not all bites will penetrate. For rabies virus to be transmitted, the skin must be broken and contaminated with saliva from the rabid animal. There have been fewer than 20 cases of confirmed rabies in ferrets in the USA since 1958; several of these were associated with vaccination of the animal with a live vaccine not approved for ferrets. Until 1992, there was no rabies vaccine approved for ferrets. The rabies vaccine labeled for ferrets is a killed virus that cannot cause rabies.

Baby ferrets born to vaccinated mothers and allowed to nurse from her for their first few days of life will be protected by the immunity in her colostrum until they are at least 9 or 10 weeks old. Rabies vaccine should be administered when the kits reach 12 weeks of age. It should not be given to younger ferrets. The ferret should have a booster every year, even if it is confined to a house or apartment. Because rabies is a highly fatal disease in all animals including man, rabies vaccine is as much for your protection as that of the animal.

Ferrets that live outside are unobserved most of the time. Although large animals such as raccoons or foxes would be noticed attacking a ferret in a cage, a bat could get through the wire and bite the ferret without anyone being aware of it. In most areas of North America, bat rabies is rare, but there are no areas where you can be absolutely sure bats are free of rabies. This is one of several good reasons not to house ferrets outside.

Some states and some cities within states categorize ferrets as wild animals, although they are not and have never been wild animals. In these areas, a ferret that bites someone, however innocently, and whether or not it has been vaccinated for rabies, will be subjected to a test for rabies. Unfortunately, the only test for rabies requires killing the animal and removing its brain. Hundreds of ferrets have been killed and rabies tested and none that were confined to homes or pet shops have been positive. The best way to avoid having your pet involved in a bite incident is not to allow strangers or even friends to handle it.

chapter 16

THREE COMMON TYPES OF CANCER IN FERRETS

LYMPHOSARCOMA

This is the most commonly diagnosed cancer in ferrets. It occurs in both old and very young ferrets. Lymphosarcoma is cancer of the lymph nodes and other lymphatic tissue such as the spleen and liver. It may or may not cause leukemia. Leukemia means that malignant white cells can be found in blood samples. Lymphosarcoma is common in other animals including man. Feline leukemia is a similar disease caused by a virus that is transmitted from the mother cat to her kittens, and from cat to cat. Bovine leukemia virus affects cattle and is mainly transmitted from cow to calf. It is likely that a virus causes lymphosarcoma in ferrets, and is passed from jills to their kits and from one pet to another. Tests that detect the feline and bovine viruses do not work in ferrets or in people. It is likely that different kinds of animals are affected by similar but different viruses. Occasionally, a disease in ferrets similar to lymphosarcoma is caused by Aleutian Disease Virus. A blood test will identify animals that have the Aleutian Disease Virus but most ferrets that test positive never show signs of illness. Blood tests, biopsies, and/or exploratory surgery are necessary to distinguish Aleutian Disease from lymphosarcoma in ferrets.

Ferrets with lymphosarcoma may seem suddenly lethargic and fail to be as active and playful as usual. They may have recurrent respiratory infections, lose weight and may have poor appetites. Often an enlarged spleen or lymph node can be felt from the outside of the animal. Your veterinarian will take a biopsy or remove a whole lymph node to make sure the enlargement is caused by cancer.

Lymphosarcoma is treatable in some animals. Chemotherapy has been successful but it is a lengthy and costly endeavor. Large tumors, for instance in the spleen, may be surgically removed, even if chemotherapy is to be used. There is no guarantee that either surgery or chemotherapy will cure the disease, but ferrets are good patients and the chemotherapy has fewer side effects in them than it does in people. Many owners feel it is well worth trying to save their little pets, and many ferrets survive and live normal lifespans afterward.

ADRENAL GLAND CANCER

Adrenal gland tumors are common in ferrets over 4 years old. The normal adrenal gland contains several types of cells that produce different hormones, such as cortisone and some male and female hormones. Excessive amounts of female hormones are often produced by adrenal gland tumors. There are no blood tests that absolutely prove that a ferret has an adrenal gland tumor because the hormones and their effects are so variable.

Possible cause of adrenal gland tumors

It has been suggested that spaying and neutering 6 to 7 week old ferrets induces adrenal gland tumors. The theory is that the adrenal glands of animals spayed or neutered very young might try to compensate for the lack of normal sex hormones by proliferation of cells that produce sex hormones. However, many ferrets spayed or neutered when much older have developed adrenal gland tumors, and occasionally animals that have not been spayed or neutered also have adrenal gland tumors. Early surgery is not the whole answer to this puzzle. Some people and animals are more susceptible to some types of cancer than others. Some ferret families may be especially susceptible to adrenal gland cancer. About 50% of unspayed jills left in heat too long will develop bone marrow hypoplasia and die, but a very small percentage of spayed animals develop adrenal tumors. The risk of not spaying is still far greater than the chance that a spayed jill will develop adrenal tumors at a young age.

Signs that a ferret has an adrenal tumor

Sometimes weight loss, hair loss, and itching for no apparent reason, are the only early signs of adrenal cancer in either a male or female ferret. Intact hobs with adrenal tumors might have permanently enlarged testicles but will be sterile. The first sign noticed by the owner of a spayed female with an adrenal gland tumor is often the sudden appearance of a swollen vulva, as if she were in heat.

Jills with hyperestrogenism

There are two common reasons for jills coming in heat long after they have been spayed. A mistake made during the spay surgery is not one of them. A jill spayed incompletely as a kit comes in heat at 4 to 6 months old depending on the hours of light each day, the same as if she were not spayed at all.

1/ Ectopic ovarian tissue. Occasionally ovarian tissue grows at the site of the spay surgery, or elsewhere in the abdomen. It is not regrowth of an ovary, it is new tissue that functions like an ovarian follicle, producing estrogen. This may happen years after the spay, for unknown reasons. If the jill is left in heat a long time, she can suffer the same side effects as with a normal estrus, including loss of hair and suppression of bone marrow. Surgical removal of the abnormal tissue immediately ends the estrus and its side effects. Injectable hormones, that work well on normal jills in heat, do not always work on jills with ectopic ovarian tissue.

2/ Adrenal gland tumors. Exploratory surgery is necessary to distinguish jills with adrenal gland tumors from those with ectopic ovarian tissue. It is possible for a jill to have both problems at once.

Prognosis for ferrets with adrenal gland tumors

If left untreated, ferrets with adrenal gland tumors usually lose all but the hair on their heads and a tuft on the tail tip. Their skin gets very thin, they have a pot-bellied appearance, and they sleep most of the time. Fortunately, although they have an odd appearance with almost no fur on their bodies, ferrets with benign adrenal gland tumors can live a reasonably normal life, if they are not anemic due to high levels of estrogen. A jill that seems to be in heat may eventually become anemic. The most effective treatment is to surgically remove the gland with the tumor. The adrenal glands produce many important substances required for life. If there are tumors on both glands, one can be removed but part of the second one must remain, even if it means leaving part of the tumor there, too. Lysodren is a drug that reduces the amount of hormone being produced by a benign inoperable tumor, extending the quality life time of the ferret. Some tumors are malignant and do not respond to Lysodren. They metastasize to other organs or recur after removal. Ferrets with malignant tumors have a short life expectancy after diagnosis.

INSULINOMAS

Insulinomas are tumors of the insulin-producing cells in the pancreas. Insulin drives blood sugar out of the blood and into body cells, making it unavailable to the brain. Ferrets with very high insulin levels appear to "faint" when their blood sugar is very low. The attacks become more frequent as the tumor or tumors grow. Very low blood sugar (hypoglycemia) causes coma and death.

Insulinomas are diagnosed by finding a low glucose level in a blood sample. Some older ferrets have both an adrenal gland tumor and insulinomas. The hormones produced by the adrenal tumor may raise blood glucose intermittently, making diagnosis more of a puzzle.

This disease usually gives the ferret a life expectancy of about a year whatever the treatment. If the tumors are very malignant, they may metastasize to other organs and shorten the animal's life to a few months. Surgical removal of all abnormal tissue that can be found causes instant improvement, but insulinomas often recur. Putting the ferret on an excellent diet and making sure it has nutritious, high-protein, low sugar snacks helps to stabilize its condition.

The best therapy for a ferret with a recently diagnosed insulinoma is removal of all visible tumors. If there are many small tumors or some that are not operable, the ferret can be put on daily prednisone, a steroid that helps to stabilize insulin levels. This will extend its quality life-time. Most ferrets will take the medication without a problem. There is another drug (diazoxide, trade name Proglycem) that stabilizes blood sugar by blocking the action of insulin, but it is very expensive and beyond the means of many owners. Neither drug will prevent metastasis nor growth of tumors.

FOR MORE INFORMATION ON . . .

hypoglycemia, see chapter 9

chapter 17

WHEN IT'S TIME TO SAY GOOD-BYE

Most of the time, people outlive their pets. Dogs and cats sometimes survive far into their teens, but ferrets rarely live more than 7 or 8 years. Eight years is not long in the life of a human being. It is more than enough time to become so attached to a favorite ferret that the thought of losing that busy, furry little body and wonderfully bright spirit is unbearably painful.

Old ferrets, and, sadly, even young ferrets, sometimes contract terminal diseases, usually cancer. Ferrets have such an optimistic outlook that they get along extremely well in the face of chemotherapy and surgery. They have a very high threshold of pain and don't appear to suffer much post-surgical discomfort. The pet-human bond becomes so strong that even a ferret that doesn't feel like eating will swallow hand-fed food for the person he loves. There comes a time when the disease has taken all his reserves. He loses weight and becomes

Old ferrets may spend most of their time sleeping, but still have a good quality life. This 7-year-old jill has had insulinomas surgically removed and is on daily medication but she eats well and enjoys human and ferret company.

skeletally thin. He barely has energy to get up to use the litter box. He sleeps most of the time, and eats only when his person of significance begs him to take one more bite. He begins to lose control of his hind legs. There is no medical treatment that will reverse all this. Your little friend tries to go on only because he knows you expect him to. He licks your face as usual, but he never does a dance of joy, never gets out of his bed unless you pick him up. You suddenly realize that you're forcing your pet to fight a battle that's already over, not because you really believe he will get well, but because you can't face losing him. He's waiting for you to let go. It's time to say good-bye.

If you've had a good relationship with your veterinarian, you can call him or her almost any time of the day or night when you've made the decision to release your friend from his struggle. Euthanasia means giving a very high dose of anesthetic, from which there is no waking. You can hold your ferret in your arms while he falls asleep for the last time. You can wrap him in his favorite bedding and cry all the way home. You can bury him with his most cherished toy in a spot you can see from your window, and plant flowers there in the spring. If you have a hundred other ferrets, you will still remember what this one meant to you. Every special ferret dances into his own place in your heart, and stays there forever.

glossary

Chapter 1

albino - an animal that is completely white because it lacks the ability to make pigment. Its eyes are pale blue or pink.

domestic animal - an animal that has been housed and fed by man for generations and has little fear of man as a result. Some domestic animals learn to depend on human provision so completely that they have little ability to survive if returned to a natural habitat.

hybrid - an animal that has parents of two different species, for instance, a mule's mother is a horse and its father is a donkey.

Mustela putorius furo - the word "furo" means "little thief", referring to the ferret's tendency to steal and hide small objects.

Chapter 2

canine distemper - a viral disease that causes a severe and often fatal systemic illness in dogs and their close relatives. Distemper is also fatal in animals such as raccoons, and mustelids including skunks, mink and ferrets.

descenting - removal of the anal sacs of a carnivore to prevent the animal from releasing the very strong-smelling secretion.

generic cat foods - foods labeled for cats and sold in grocery stores, having ground yellow corn as the major ingredient and often lacking one or more nutrients essential to cats and ferrets. These foods usually have not undergone testing in animals.

neuter - sterilization by surgical removal of the testicles of a male animal.

nocturnal - animals that are active during the night and sleep during the day.

spay - sterilization by surgical removal of the ovaries and uterus of a female animal.

vaccination - administration of live or killed organisms (viruses, bacteria or parasites) to induce immunity in an animal. Live organisms are modified so that they do not cause disease in the species of animal for which the vaccine is intended, but the same vaccine might cause illness in another species of animal more susceptible to the disease.

Chapter 3

carnivore - an animal whose natural diet includes meat.

coma - an unconscious, unresponsive state caused by brain dysfunction.

convulsion - uncontrolled movements ("fits") due to abnormal brain function.

predator - an animal that kills birds, fish or other animals for food.

prey - living creatures that are hunted and killed for food.

vermin - small wild animals, such as squirrels, groundhogs and rabbits, that are hunted and killed because humans consider them harmful or unnecessary.

Chapter 5

chronic illness - a disease that persists for weeks or months, and possibly for the life of the animal, due to lack of treatment or the incurable nature of the disease.

Chapter 6

calorie - the unit of measurement of energy derived from digested food. Fat contains about twice as many calories per gram as protein or carbohydrate.

carbohydrate - compounds made up of chains of sugar units. Simple carbohydrates include table sugar (sucrose), milk sugar (lactose), and fruit sugar (fructose). Complex carbohydrates are very long chains held together by bonds that may not be digestible in the stomach and intestine of a carnivore. Starch is a digestible complex carbohydrate. Seed hulls such as oat bran are digestible by ruminants and horses but not carnivores.

diabetes - a metabolic disease caused by failure of the pancreas to produce insulin, a hormone that allows blood sugar (glucose) to be taken up by cells that require it for function.

malnutrition - ill health due to a dietary deficiency or imbalance.

microorganism - a single-celled life form that is invisible to the naked eye and that may cause disease in man or animals.

nutrient - a chemical, categorized as fat, protein, carbohydrate, mineral, vitamin or water, required by an animal to maintain its weight, health and activity

obligate carnivore - an animal that requires in its diet nutrients that are found in sufficient quantities only in meat or other animal products.

plaque - a build-up of bacteria and minerals on the teeth, forming a hard coating and eventually causing gum disease and tooth loss.

premium cat foods - cat food specifically formulated to meet the nutrient requirements of cats, with meat the major ingredient.

Premium cat foods are sold in pet and specialty shops, and sometimes by veterinarians. These products have undergone testing in cats to confirm their nutritional value and palatability.

Chapter 7

semi-moist cat/ferret treat - packaged food made from very palatable meat or fish products, and with a high moisture content (e.g. 30% compared to 10% for dry pellets).

Chapter 8

ear canal - the tube that connects the external ear with the ear drum.

ear drum - the membrane that divides the outer ear from the inner ear, where the mechanism of hearing takes place. The membrane prevents infection from reaching the inner ear, as well as vibrating to amplify sounds.

ear mites - small parasitic insects that live in the ear canal of an animal, and that are able to survive outside the ear for only very short periods of time.

flea dip - a solution made to kill fleas, applied to an animal and not rinsed off, to allow it to have residual action.

innate - a permanent characteristic that is present because of the genetic make-up of the animal.

Chapter 9

alopecia - loss of hair leaving the skin exposed.

anaphylaxis - a very rapid allergic reaction to an injected, swallowed, or applied substance that causes collapse in some animals and difficulty breathing in others. Spontaneous recovery may occur but it is a potentially fatal reaction when severe.

balanced electrolytes - salt solution similar in nature to the liquid part of the blood.

BUN - short for "blood urea nitrogen", a blood test that estimates kidney function.

dehydration - loss of body fluids because of lack of drinking water, diarrhea, or vomiting. Causes loss of elasticity of the skin, dryness of the mouth and eyes. Severe dehydration reduces blood volume, and the animal will collapse and die if the fluids are not replaced.

estrus - the time when a female animal is fertile and receptive to the male. Also known as a heat period.

gram - a measure of weight. 28 grams = 1 oz, 454 grams = 1 lb.

insulin - a hormone produced by the pancreas, that allows blood glucose to be taken into cells and used for energy.

heartworm - a species of parasitic worm that lives and reproduces in the chambers of the heart of an animal. Microsopic, immature worms (microfilariae) circulate in the blood and are taken in by mosquitoes that bite the animal. Microfilariae mature in the mouthparts of the mosquito and infect another susceptible animal bitten by the same mosquito.

hypoglycemia - low blood sugar causing brain dysfunction and weakness.

ml - short for milliliter. A liquid measure, the same volume as a cc. 28 ml = 1 liquid oz.

ovulation - rupture of the follicle on an ovary, releasing an egg, and allowing fertilization. Production of estrogen by the follicle stops after ovulation.

photoperiod - the number of hours of light per 24-hour period.

rabies - a fatal virus disease of warm blooded animals including man, that affects the brain and is spread in the saliva of infected animals. Rabid animals have a temperament change. Wild creatures become bold enough to attack human beings, and docile domestic animals may turn on their owners.

sarcoptic mange - a skin disease induced by a parasitic mite that lives in the skin, causing irritation and itching. Affects man, dogs and their relatives, mustelids and other animals.

Chapter 10

exotic - an animal not native to the geographical area where it is living.

Chapter 11

cataract - a cloudiness of the lens of the eye, reducing vision and giving the eye a pearly appearance.

congenital - a characteristic of an animal that is present at birth. It may be inherited or induced by events that occur during pregnancy.

estrogen - a female hormone produced by the ovaries, in a ferret causing swelling of the vulva and receptivity to the male.

inherited - a trait passed from one generation to the next in the genes from each parent.

Chapter 12

acid - a fluid containing a high proportion of hydrogen ions, giving the liquid a sour taste. Measured by pH units, with 1 the most acid, and 14 the least acid. Chemical reactions in the body have to take place at or near neutrality, pH 7.

alkaline - a substance with very few hydrogen ions, and a pH over 7. Lye is strongly alkaline.

anorexia - lack of appetite.

by-products - ground up animal tissue that might include indigestible parts such as tendons, and food of low nutritional value such as lungs.

cecum - a blind sac that opens into the colon of many animals. Not present in the mustelid's intestine.

digestibility - expressed as a percent, is a measure of the content of food that is retained in the body after food is eaten. The difference between the weight of food eaten and the weight of stool produced, divided by the weight of the food.

large intestine - the lower part of the intestinal tract, usually made up of the colon, cecum and rectum. Bacteria that live harmlessly in the large intestine help to digest complex carbohydrates.

meal - when referring to food ingredients, means a ground-up preparation. Chicken meal is ground up chicken, which might include bones and feathers. Meat meal means ground up muscle meat.

struvite - magnesium ammonium phosphate, a compound that forms crystals in an alkaline medium, and dissolves in an acid medium. A common component of bladder stones in cats and ferrets.

Chapter 13

immunodeficiency - reduced function of the immune system of an animal, making it more susceptible to infectious disease. Can be an inherited defect or caused by drugs, radiation or viruses.

immunosuppressive - something, for instance a drug, hormone or virus, that reduces the function of the immune system of an animal.

larva - the worm-like offspring of an insect (plural larvae).

microfilaria - the larval form of some parasitic worms, for example heartworms. These worms do not lay eggs, they produce microfilariae instead.

offal - animal organs rejected at slaughter as unfit for human consumption, e.g spleen, intestine, brain, lungs.

otic - pertaining to the ear.

protozoans - single-celled animals invisible to the naked eye. Most are free living and a few are parasites in animals or man.

Chapter 14

pupa - a dormant form of an insect (plural pupae). A larva spins a cocoon to protect itself, and becomes a pupa. The pupa does not feed but gradually changes form and becomes a new adult.

Chapter 14

colitis - inflammation of the lining of the colon, part of the large intestine.

gastritis - inflammation of the lining of the stomach.

prolapsed rectum - because of irritation or injury, the inner part of the rectum is pushed out so that it is visible as a pink mass protruding from the anal opening.

virus - the smallest form of life, invisible with an ordinary microscope. An infectious unit that enters and uses cells of plants or animals for replication. Some viruses cause disease in animals or plants.

wasting - loss of muscle mass due to decreased food intake or increased metabolic rate.

Chapter 16

adrenal glands - two small glands near the kidneys that produce many hormones required for life. Removal of both adrenal glands causes death.

benign - referring to non-cancerous tumors, growths that are relatively harmless and slow-growing, and do not spread to near-by or distant organs.

biopsy - surgical removal of a small amount of abnormal tissue, usually of tumors, for diagnosis.

ectopic - non-malignant tissue growing in an unusual location (e.g., an ectopic pregnancy is conception of a normal embryo outside the normal location, which is the uterus).

liver - the largest organ in the abdomen, responsible for producing enzymes required for digestion of food, and bile that helps to digest fat. The liver also detoxifies the blood and may be damaged in the process.

lymph nodes - part of the immune system of an animal. Small masses of tissue that contain white blood cells called lymphocytes. Blood from the nearby area is filtered through the lymph node allowing foreign or infectious material to be recognized and destroyed if possible.

malignant - a process that does harm to nearby tissues. Usually synonymous with cancer, a tumor that grows quickly and spreads both in the original area where it occurred and in remote parts of the body.

metastasis - spread of a tumor from its original location to a remote one, by tumor cells that are carried in the blood.

spleen - part of the immune system of an animal. A large tongue-shaped organ in the abdomen containing many lymphocytes. The spleen filters blood and removes damaged cells. It can also manufacture new blood cells if the animal's bone marrow is damaged.

appendix A

MEDICATIONS COMMONLY USED IN FERRETS

This is not intended to be an exhaustive list. It will make you familiar with many drugs prescribed for ferrets by veterinarians. It is never wise to use a medication prescribed for another animal to treat a ferret that seems to have the same problem. The problem may not actually be the same, and dosages must be calculated on a body weight basis. Drug interactions can cause complex and sometimes harmful results. There are no drugs specifically labeled for use in ferrets.

Antibiotics

AMOXICILLIN: Oral suspension is palatable and easy to give. Trade names include Amoxi Drops, Biomox, Robamox and a related drug, Clavamox. Used mainly for respiratory infections and gastric ulcers. May (rarely) cause hypoglycemia, ferret may convulse or become very weak, give corn syrup if animal is conscious.

TRIMETHOPRIM SULFA: Oral suspension is palatable and easy to give. Trade names include Ditrim, Sulfatrim, Bactrim, SMZ-TMP, Tribrissen. Used for bladder infections, respiratory infections, skin infections including mastitis, and coccidiosis.

CEPHALOTHINS : Oral suspensions, palatable and easy to give, several related drugs, e.g., trade name Cefa Drops. Used for upper respiratory infections, mastitis.

BAYTRIL (trade name): Tablets and injectable, used for respiratory infections. Should not be given to growing animals, may interfere with bone development.

TETRACYCLINE: Oral suspension, trade name Aquadrops, used for respiratory and skin infections. CAN DAMAGE THE TOOTH ENAMEL OF KITS UNDER 11 WEEKS, MAY INTERFERE WITH BONE GROWTH, SHOULD NOT USE IN PREGNANT JILLS.

CHLORAMPHENICOL: Trade name Chloromycetin palmitate, tablet and injectable forms, the only effective drug for proliferative colitis. Tablets may be made into a suspension by a pharmacist to make ferret treatment easier. Generally safe in ferrets, rarely induces hypoglycemia, BUT VERY DANGEROUS FOR SOME PEOPLE, USE CAUTION WHEN DOSING YOUR FERRET, AVOID SKIN CONTACT.

METRONIDAZOLE: Tablets, trade name Flagyl, have to be ground up to get the proper dose for a ferret. Bitter taste, hard to give. Used for gastritis and ulcers caused by *Helicobacter mustelae* , and for giardiasis.

GENTACIN: SHOULD NEVER BE GIVEN TO A FERRET, MAY INDUCE FATAL KIDNEY DAMAGE. ALSO CAUSES DEAFNESS IN FERRETS.

Other Drugs

PEPTO BISMOL: for diarrhea, especially caused by gastritis, ulcers. CONTAINS SALICYLATES WHICH CAN BE TOXIC. Ferret should not get more than 8 mg/lb body weight daily.

PANALOG, DERMAVET, other trade names. Oily yellow suspension used to treat ear and skin infections. Contains cortisone, should never be used in a pregnant jill, could cause birth defects or abortion.

IVERMECTIN: Tablets (Heartguard) for heartworm prevention, injectable (Ivomec) can also be used orally as heartworm preventive and for eosinophilic gastroenteritis, or mixed with bland oil and used to treat the ear canal for mites.

EAR MITE REMEDIES: products safe for cats include trade names Mitaban, Mitox, Aurimite, Cerumite, or any others containing rotenone or pyrethrins.

PYRETHRINS, PERMETHRINS: chemicals included in flea sprays, shampoos and dips, safe for ferrets. Permethrins are longer acting. Both also kill ear mites and ticks.

PREDNISOLONE: Prednisone tablets and syrups such as Pediapred, Prelone. A steroid similar to cortisone, used to stabilize blood sugar in ferrets with insulinomas, to treat lymphosarcoma and eosinophilic gastroenteritis, and after adrenal gland surgery.

DIAZOXIDE: Oral suspension, trade name Proglycem. Used to block the action of insulin in ferrets with inoperable insulinomas. Very expensive.

MITOTANE: Capsules, trade name Lysodren. Used for inoperable benign adrenal tumors. Cannot be used in ferrets with insulinomas.

GnRH (gonadotrophin releasing hormone) and **hCG** (human chorionic gonadotrophin): injectable hormones used to induce ovulation in jills. HCG may induce allergic reactions and will become ineffective if used several times in the same animal. Neither drug will work until the jill has been in heat for 10 days.

Vaccines

CANINE DISTEMPER VACCINES: the only safe vaccines for ferrets are FERVAC-D (United Vaccines) and mink vaccines such as DISTEMINK (United Vaccines) and DISTEM-R (Schering). All are modified live vaccines produced in egg embryo tissue cultures, not stable line cell cultures. All stable line cell culture vaccines intended for dogs can produce distemper in ferrets. Killed vaccines do not protect ferrets.
RABIES VACCINES: only killed vaccines should be used. There is one labeled for ferrets, IMRAB3 (Rhone Merieux). Imrab1 is safe but is not approved for ferrets. Live vaccines have produced rabies in ferrets and should never be used.

appendix B

AREAS WHERE PET FERRETS ARE ILLEGAL

It is illegal to keep ferrets as pets in California, Massachusetts, Hawaii, and the District of Columbia. There are also some municipal areas or counties in other states where they are illegal.

Because of the confusion about whether ferrets are domestic animals like cats, or exotic animals, some other areas outlaw ferret ownership depending on the local ordinances regarding exotic pets. Occasionally ferrets are even considered "wild" animals, although they were developed as a domestic species and there never were any wild ones. Before you adopt a ferret, find out about the laws in your own area. Local ferret clubs are the best source of information. If you cannot locate a ferret club, inquire of the American Ferret Association. Licenses are required in some states, such as New York, or some areas within states. In these areas, pet shops that sell ferrets will have the forms to apply for a license, and will not sell you a ferret until you have the license in your hand.

appendix C

RESOURCES FOR FERRET OWNERS

There are many local ferret clubs across the US and Canada, some associated with shelters and some just groups of ferret owners who meet, compare notes, listen to expert speakers occasionally, and possibly hold small shows once a year. Some publish regular newsletters giving members information about ferret diseases, upcoming events, or political news about areas that have banned ferrets or released ferrets from a ban. The American Ferret Association is a national group that publishes an excellent bi-monthly report. Local chapters meet independently. Because the group has a very large membership and an active executive, there is little that happens in the ferret world that escapes the AFA.

To join the American Ferret Association, write to :

American Ferret Association, Inc.
PO Box 3986
Frederick, MD 21705

The advantages of being a member include access to useful information for ferret owners, such as finding a nearby veterinarian who is experienced in treating ferrets, or dates and locations of upcoming shows, as well as legal concerns such as the need for a license in your area, or the local policy regarding disposition of "stray" ferrets.

The following list of ferret shelters, courtesy of the American Ferret Association, is no doubt incomplete, but calling the nearest one will put you in touch with a network of ferret owners who can answer your questions.

ferret shelters

Alabama
Gulf Coast Ferret Rescue
Director: Marty Loeffler
Chicksaw, AL (205)457-8346

Arizona
Adopt-A-Ferret
Director: Judi Sears
Tucson, AZ (602)326-8439

Central Arizona Ferret Club/Shelter
Director: Suzanne & Ken Resinger
Phoenix, AZ (602)840-0813

Ferret Friends
Director: Ginny Childs
Tucson, AZ (602) 622-4940

Heartbeat Ferrets
Directors: Helen White & Dan McCulloch
Glendale, AZ (602) 435-9440

California
California Domestic Ferret Association
Director: Bill Phillips
Healdsburg, CA (707) 431-2277

CANADA
Canadian Ferret Association/Shelter
Director: Heather Dodge
(604) 534-4150

Delta Ferret Rescue
Tracey Lee rein
Delat, British Columbia
(601) 943-8149

Colorado
Colorado Ferret Rescue
Director: R.A. Yaroush
Boulder, CO (303) 444-7364

Colorado Ferret Rescue
Director: Scotti Pelhan
Littleton, CO (303) 972-3316

Ferret Rescue of the Western States
Director: Carol Kinsey
2809 Lucas Ave
Pueblo, CO 81005

Connecticut
Ferret Assoc. of Connecticut
Directors: Ann & Vanessa Gruden
Hartford, CT (203) 247-1275

Delaware
Delaware Halfway House
Director: Steve Krouse
(302) 633-1308

DVFC Shelter & Rescue
Director: Cindy Sooy
Newark, DE (302) 738-0115

Florida
Brevard Ferret Rescue
Director: Sandy Cordova
Palm Bay, FL (407) 728-8698

C-Treasures Ferret Rescue
Director: Debbie Coburn
Orlando, FL (407) 380-8712

Ferret Connection
Director: Mary Lou Johnson
Ft. Myers Beach, FL (813) 466-8900

Ferret Alfonso Ferret Rescue Ctr.
Director: Joanne Fisher
Jensen Beach, FL. (407) 334-4130

Gainesville Ferret Meisters
Gainesville, FL (904) 377-1382

Miami Ferret Club, Inc./Shelter
Director: Angela Espinet
Miami, FL (305) 251-8647

Suncoast Weasel Waystation
Director: Steve Boyce
St. Petersberg, FL (813) 541-4918

Georgia
GA Domestic Ferret Assoc/Shelter
Director: Jan Lovell
Cumming, GA (404) 442-5917

Illinois
Central Illinois Friends of Ferrets
Director: Kathy Fritz
Champaign, IL. (217) 356-6063

Ferret Adoption, Info & Rescue Society
Director: Mary K. Van Dahm
Westmont, IL (708) 968-3189

Greater Chicago Ferret Shelter
Westmont, IL (708) 964-4232

Indiana
Ferret Rescue & Halfway House
Martinsville, IN (765) 349-0265
Contact: Mason Lowrey

Iowa
East Iowa Ferret Assoc/Shelter
Director: Dr. Fitzgerald
West Branch, IA (319) 646-6028

Kansas
Ferret Family Services
Director: Troy Lynn Eckart
Manhattan, KS (913) 494-8415

Maine
Halfway House For Ferrets
Director: Joanne Calderbank
Westbrook, ME (207) 856-6568

Mainely Mustelids
Director: Lynn Hendrickson
Bath, ME (207) 442-0998

Maryland
All About Bandit
Director: Carol & Jim Scott
Crownsville, MD (410) 932-2417

Carroll County Ferret Rescue
Director: Terry Fike
Taneytown, MD (410) 751-1526

Fran's Ferret Rescue
Director: Fran Wiles
Smithsburg, MD (301) 416-0606

Howard County Ferret Shelter
Directors: Lucia & David Ditch
Laurel, MD (301) 776-8841

Metro Ferret Rescue League
Directors: Denise Edens/Ellen Byrne
Germantown, MD (301) 972-1618
or (301) 540-2756

Massachusetts
Michael Alfonso Ferret Rescue Ctr.
Director: Bruce Deane White
Assonet, MA (508) 644-3131
or (508) 644-5562

Minnesota
D.E.F.F.B.A.M.
Director: Joel Johnson
St. Paul, MN (612) 433-3266

Mississippi
Wreaking Crew - Shelter
Director: Wade Moates
Ocean springs, MS (601) 875-8927

Missouri
Ferret Referral Services/Rescue
Director: Leah & Jim Harrington
Jennings, MO (314) 382-6327

Nevada
Nevada Ferret Assoc/Shelter
Director: Lynn Schultz
Las Vegas, NV (702) 870-9677

New Hampshire
Four Lil' Paws Ferret Rescue
Directors: Dick & Joan Bossart
Merrimack, NH (603) 424-2941

New Jersey
Itty Bitty Critter Rescue
Directors: Richard & Nancy Joyce
Toms River, NJ (908) 341-6960

New Jersey Ferret Assoc/Shelter
Director: Sandy Stillwell
Hamilton Sq., NJ (609) 586-6962

North West Jersey Ferret Haven
Director: Jane Casale
Ogdensburg, NJ (201) 827-5170

New York
Ferret Shelter
Director: Guy Antonelli
68 Meadow Hill Rd
Newburg, NY 12550

Little Thieves Rescue
Director: Thomas Ievoli
Kings Park, NY (516) 269-7236

Western NY & Finger Lakes Ferret Assoc
Director: Deborah J. Riccio
Rochester, NY (716) 473-7292

Woodland Sprite Ferret Shelter
Director: Patricia Savoie
Amsterdam, NY (518) 842-3820

Ohio
Ferrets Dream House
Director: Lori Sies
3973 Elljay Drive
Cincinnati, OH. (513) 733-8167

Ferret Sense
Director: Linda Harrah
Buckeye Lake, OH (614) 929-3392

Oregon
Dragonlyn Acres
Director: Trisha Hellbronn
North Bend, OR (503) 756-1166

Oregon Ferret Assoc. Shelter/Rescue
Directors: David & Christine Mathis
Portland, OR (503) 557-8369

Pennsylvania
Central Berks Ferret Rescue
Directors: Clarence & Shirley Hertzog
Shillington, PA (215) 777-3329

Central PA Ferret Rescue
Director: Kymberlie Becker
State College, PA (814) 867-8562

Ferret Connection Rescue
Director: Tracy McAlister
Bridgeville, PA (412) 221-2314

The Ferret Gallery
Directors: Chris & Cheryl Goedeke
Harleysville, PA. (215) 256-1164

Legion of Superferrets
Director: Rose Smith
Levittown, PA (215) 946-2747

Montgomery Ferret Rescue
Director: Desiree Kehr
Hatfield, PA (215) 368-3906

Oxford Ferret Rescue
Director: Samantha Benson
Oxford, PA (215) 932-5463

Schuylkill County Ferret Rescue
Director: Beth Schwenk
New Ringgold, PA (717) 943-7683

Susquehanna Valley Ferret Rescue
Director: Jodi Schroth
Harrisburg, PA (717) 540-1078

Triple C Ferrets
Director: Lynda & Jay Church
Warren, PA (814) 723-1050

South Carolina
Katie's Rescue & Shelter
Director: Katie Sweeney
Greenville, SC (803) 322-6111

Tennessee
Tennessee Valley Ferret Club/Rescue
Director: Bob & Gina Eaton
Soddy Daisy, TN (615) 843-1786

Texas
Ferret Lover's Club
Director: Karen Grant
Bedford, TX (817) 545-0649

San Antonio Ferrret Enthusiasts
Directors: Rick & Candi White
Kirby, TX (210) 661-9195

Schermerhorn's Shelter
Director: Sharon Schermerhorn
Austin, TX (512) 453-8597

Weasel Way Station
Director: Ann Holman
Bryan, TX (409) 589-2870

Virginia
Dragon Run Ferrets & Rescue
Director: Georgia Bailey
Newport News, VA (804) 887-5688

Washington
Ferrets Northwest Shelter & Rescue
Director: Ed Lipinski
Mercer Island, WA (206) 232-1228

Ferrets Northwest - Tacoma
Director: Bobbi Younce
Tacoma, WA (206) 584-5266

Wisconsin
Ferret Fanciers of Greater Milwaukee
PO BOx 11625
Milwaukee, WI 53211

Ferret Foundlings
Director: Karen Yaremkowych
Horicon, WI (414) 485-2512

index

Accidents
household 10, 12, 13, 20
outside 13, 22, 37
Adrenal gland tumor 17, 34, 56, 61, 62
estrogen production 34
hair loss 33, 34
itching 34, 56
swollen vulva 34, 56
AIDS
Cryptosporidiosis 47
Air travel
upper respiratory infections 37, 50
Aleutian Disease 56
Allergies 50
cedar 49
fleas 49
food 34
to vaccines 30, 31, 60
American Ferret Association 63
Anal sacs (musk glands)
function of 6, 15, 31, 32
Anemia
fleas 21, 49
with adrenal tumors 57
with prolonged estrus 31, 40
Animal shelters/pounds 13
ferret policy 13, 63
Antibiotics 62
hypoglycemia 34
upper respiratory infections 21, 35, 50
wasting diseases 52, 62
Apartment living 9, 12
Appetite, loss of (anorexia)
feeding 46
hairballs 53
Helicobacter mustelae 5, 52
lymphosarcoma 56
Babies (see kits) 6
Baldness (see hair loss) 33
Bathing
frequency 27
shampoos 27, 34
technique 27, 28, 34
to control fleas 27, 49

when shedding 53
Beds (see nests) 21, 22
Behavior 9, 12-16, 18, 19, 25, 26
digging 12, 26, 29
nests 9, 10, 21, 22
Birds 13, 15
Birthing problems 40, 42
Biting 9, 10
children 13
fear reaction 15
jills with babies 16
juvenile 16
kits 15, 16
strangers 10, 37
test for rabies 10, 37, 55
ways to release 16
when hurt 10
when scruffed 28
Black-footed ferret 6
Black stool
ulcers 51
Bladder stones
due to infection 31, 40, 45
on poor diet 43, 44, 45, 61
Blindness
cataracts 42
distinguish from exhuberance 15
hypoglycemia 34
Blood test
for adrenal gland tumor 56
for Aleutian disease 56
for eosinophilic gastroenteritis 53
for glucose (sugar) 31, 57
for heartworms 47, 48
for kidney problems 31, 52, 60
for leukemia (lymphosarcoma) 31, 56
Blue skin
with hair regrowth 33
Boarding
at veterinary hospitals 38
Bordetella bronchiseptica 38, 50
suitable for ferrets 38
upper respiratory infections 38, 50

Bone marrow hypoplasia
jills in heat 31, 40, 57
with adrenal tumors 57
Bordetella bronchiseptica 38, 50
vaccination 38, 50
Breeding 41, 44
Breeding season 40
hours of light 18, 31, 40
Buying a ferret
from a pet shop 17
from a shelter 18, 19
from a small breeder 18, 52
Cages 8, 9, 10, 24
in veterinary hospitals 38
outside 22, 34, 55
Calories required daily 44, 46
Cancer 10, 31, 56, 57, 61
adrenal gland tumors 17, 33, 34, 56, 57
insulinomas 31, 45, 57
lymphosarcoma 56
Canned cat food 44
Carbohydrates in ferret diets 23, 44, 59
Cardiomyopathy 47
Carnivore 6, 23
Castration (see neutering) 31
Cat food 38, 44
generic 10, 23, 34, 43, 44, 45, 59
premium 23, 44, 45, 47, 59
Cataracts 42, 60
Cats 12, 13
ear mites 28, 29, 48
flea control products 49
fleas 21
in boarding kennels 38
Cedar litter
allergies 49
flea control 26, 27, 49
Chemotherapy
for lymphosarcoma 56
Children
and ferrets 6, 13
Claws (see nails) 29
Coat colors
albino 7, 42, 59

black sable	7
black-eyed whites	7
butterscotch	7
chocolate	7
cinnamon	7
pandas	7
sable	7
Siamese	7
silver	7
silver mitt	7

Coat conditioner (linoleic acid)
Ferrotone, Linotone	24, 25, 34

Coccidiosis 35, 47
diarrhea	47, 51
stool sample to diagnose	30, 47, 51
treatment	47, 62

Colds 21, 35, 38, 39
treatment	21, 35, 45

Colitis (see proliferative colitis) 51, 52

Colostrum
protection against distemper	54
protection against rabies	54

Coma 57, 59
due to Bordetella	50
due to hypoglycemia	34, 57
sound sleepers	14

Convulsions 14, 15, 59
Bordetella bronchiseptica	50
caused by hypoglycemia	34
distemper	54

Corona virus diarrhea (see green slime disease)
sources of infection	37, 52

Cryptosporidium parvum 47

Daily care
minimum	9, 10
to minimize odor	27

Declawing 29

Deafness 34, 62

Defects (congenital) 41, 42, 60
cataracts	42, 60
cystic kidneys	42
extra toes	42
pug faces	32, 33, 42

Dehydration 47, 50, 60
corona virus diarrhea	52
distemper	54
electrolytes	47
foreign bodies	53

wasting diseases	52

Descenting 10
effects of	27, 31, 35, 59
surgical procedure	31, 32, 35

Diabetes 24

Diarrhea 35, 50-52
bacterial	51
bloody	35, 47, 51
caused by laxative	35, 53
coccidiosis	47, 51
dairy products	24, 35, 50
dehydration	35, 47
eosinophilic gastroenteritis	53
green mucus	51
Helicobacter mustelae gastritis	51
infectious	37, 51
nutritional	23, 50
parasitic	60
proliferative colitis	51
viral, "green slime disease"	37, 52

Diet (see Food) 10, 23, 24, 35, 43-46

Digestive tract 43, 44

Digging 12, 26, 29

Dirofilaria immitis (see heartworm)

Distemper (Canine) 10, 30, 59
carriers	21, 30, 59
exposure	18, 40
hard pads	54
modified live vaccines	54, 62
passive immunity	54
sources of infection	21, 30, 37, 38, 54
swollen rectum	54
vaccination	10, 21, 30, 37, 38, 54

Distemper vaccines
allergic reaction to	30
for dogs	54
for ferrets	54, 62
for mink	54

Dog food 10, 23

Dogs 12, 13
Bordetella bacterin	38, 50
Bordetella bronchiseptica	38
distemper	21, 30, 54, 59
ear mites	28, 29, 48
fleas	21
in boarding kennels	38
sarcoptic mange	34, 60

Drooling 35

Ear cleaning 28

Ear infections 28, 29

Ear mites 28, 29, 48, 60
treatment	29, 48, 62

Electrolytes
for diarrhea	35, 47, 52, 60

Emergencies 34, 35, 47, 52
Diarrhea	35
Heat stroke	22, 34
Hypoglycemia	31, 34, 35, 37, 45, 57
Prolapsed rectum	32, 35
Respiratory infections	35
Vomiting	35

Eosinophilic gastroenteritis 52

Estrogen, effects of 31, 33, 34, 40, 57, 60

Euthanasia 58

Exercise 3, 5, 8, 9, 10, 14

Fat requirement 44

Fear reaction 15

Feeding
babies	44, 45
cost	10
during pregnancy & lactation	44, 45
feed containers	22, 24
ferrets with insulinomas	35, 45
how to feed	24, 52
need for water	22, 24, 45, 51
outside	22, 24
sick ferrets	35, 45, 46, 47, 52
what to feed	10, 23, 24, 43
when boarding	38
when travelling	37, 38

Ferret behavior 4

Ferret odor
during breeding season	27, 31, 32, 40
descenting	27, 31

Ferret owners 6

Ferret shelters 18, 19, 37, 64, 65

Ferret shows 19, 39
distemper vaccination	39
infectious disease	19, 39, 52
stress	50

Ferret-proofing 12, 20

Ferrets
and cats	9
and children	8
and dogs	9
and other small pets	13

Black-footed 1
lifespan 8, 10, 58
Mustela putorius furo 6, 59
used for hunting 6
Ferrotone (linoleic acid) 24, 25
for itchy skin 34
as training aid 25
for nail trimming 29
Fighting (with other ferrets) 14, 31
First Aid 34
Fish in diet 23
Flea control 27, 49, 62
cedar litter 26
dips 27, 28, 49, 60, 62
shampoos 27, 49, 62
Fleas 21, 49
allergies 49
anemia 21, 49
itching 33, 49
Flu (see influenza)
Food - good diet (see also Feeding)
animal fat required 44
benefits of pelleted food 24, 32
caloric content 44
containers/dishes 21, 22, 24
crude protein requirement 44
for ferrets 23, 43
guaranteed analysis 44
high quality premium cat food 23, 59
importance of palatability 23, 38
important to health 10, 23, 43
must contain meat 23, 43
proper storage 24
when nursing kits 51
when pregnant 51
Food - poor diet
cause of bladder stones 43, 45
cause of dry itchy skin 33, 34
dog food 10, 23
effect of soft food on teeth 24, 32, 44
generic cat food 10, 23, 34, 43, 59
ground yellow corn 43
moldy food 24
raw meat 23, 47
stress 20, 51
Foreign bodies 25, 50, 53
intestinal blockage 53
rubber 53

Giardia lamblia 47, 54, 62
in humans 47
Gibs 6
Green diarrhea (corona virus) 37, 52
Green mucus 51, 52
proliferative colitis 50, 51
Hair loss (alopecia) 60
adrenal gland tumor 17, 33, 34, 56, 57
seasonal 27, 33, 53
slow growth after clipping 33
tail alopecia 33
with prolonged heat periods 3, 33, 57
Hairballs
prevention 53
shedding 27, 53
treatment 35, 53
Hammocks 10, 22
Harnesses suitable for ferrets 37
Heartworm 22, 47, 60
blood test 48
microfilaria 48, 60
prevention 31, 48, 62
treatment 48
Heat (estrus) 60
controlling 31, 40
due to adrenal gland tumor 33, 34, 57
due to ectopic ovarian tissue 57
prolonged 31, 33, 40, 57
seasonal 27, 40
signs of 31, 34, 40
Heat stroke
ferret sensitivity 13, 22, 37
treatment 34
Helicobacter mustelae gastritis 51, 52
Hind leg weakness/paralysis 15, 38, 58
Hobs 6
greasy skin 28, 31
Hormones 56
for ectopic ovarian tissue 57
growth-stimulating effect 31
to induce ovulation 40, 62
Housing
in groups 9, 14, 22, 31
outside 20, 22, 31, 34, 48, 55
room temperature 22
Hypoglycemia 31, 60
signs 34, 57
treatment 34, 35, 45, 57

Illegal status 18, 37, 38
states that forbid ferrets 37, 38, 63
Influenza 50
exposure 37, 50
treatment 37
Inherited defects
cataracts 42
cystic kidneys 42
extra toes (polydactyly) 42
"pug" faces (brachycephaly) 42
Insulinomas 31, 34, 57, 62
dietary requirement 45, 57
Intestinal obstruction
rubber 25, 53
treatment 53
Itching 15
adrenal gland tumor 34, 58
due to allergies 34
due to low fat diet 34, 44
due to sarcoptic mange 34
due to shampooing 27, 33
fleas 33, 49
Jills 6
Juveniles
behavior 14, 15, 16
biting 15, 16
Kits 6, 41
behavior 8, 21
birth defects 32, 33, 42
care required 21
coccidiosis 47, 51
colds 21, 50
color at birth 7
cryptosporidiosis 7
distemper vaccination 21, 54
fear reaction 15
fleas 21
food requirement 46
growth rate 41, 44
hand feeding 45
litter training 26
play-biting 15
teething 32, 41
veterinary care required 21
weaning age 32, 41, 44
Laxative for hairballs 27, 35, 36, 53
Leashes suitable for ferrets 37, 41

Leukemia 56
Licenses 10
Light, hours of (photoperiod)
  effect on coat 27, 33, 53
  effect on estrus 40, 41, 60
Linotone (linoleic acid) (see Ferretone)
  as training aid 25
  for nail trimming 29
Litter
  cedar 26, 49
  clay 26
  clumping 26
  dusty 26
  paper 26
  perfumed 26
  recycled paper 26
  wood products 26
Litter box 15, 26, 35, 51
  cleaning 8, 26, 35, 47, 49, 51
  disposable 38, 42
  suitable for ferrets 25, 26
  types of litter 26, 49
Litter size 41, 44
Litter training 9, 21, 26, 45
Low blood sugar (see hypoglycemia)
Lymphosarcoma 52, 56
Lysodren, for adrenal tumors 57
Mange, sarcoptic 34
Microfilaria, heartworm 48
Mink 6, 23, 54
Molting (see shedding)
Musk glands
  descenting 27, 31, 32, 59
  fear reaction 15, 31, 32
  odor 27, 31, 32
Mustela putorius furo
  domestic ferret 6, 59
Mustelids 6, 31
  canine distemper 54, 59
  coccidiosis 47
  mange 60
Nail trimming 29
Nests
  types 10, 21, 22
  when boarding 38
Neutering (castration) 31, 40, 59
  age to do 17, 31
  effects of 27, 31, 56

New ferrets, introducing to group 14
Nutrition (see Food) 43-46
Nutritional supplements
  Ferrotone, Linotone 24, 25, 29, 34, 36
  for babies 45
  for sick ferrets 35, 36, 44, 45, 46, 52
Odor (see ferret odor) 27
Oocysts (eggs) coccidia 47
Otodectes cynotes (ear mites) 48
Outside exercise 9
  risks 13, 21, 37, 38
Outside housing
  heartworm prevention 31, 48
  rabies 55
  risks 13, 22, 34, 54, 55
Overcrowding 50, 51
Ovulation 31
  induced by hormones 40, 57, 62
Parasites (external) 49
  ear mites 48
  fleas 49
Parasites (internal)
  coccidia 47
  Cryptosporidium parvum 47
  Giardia lamblia 47
  heartworms 47, 48
  protozoans 47
  worms 47
Passive immunity
  colostrum 54
  distemper 54
  rabies 54
Pet shops
  source of ferret diets 10, 23
  source of ferret licenses 63
  source of ferrets 17-19
  stressful conditions 20, 21, 50
Playfulness 8, 9, 13, 25, 26
Polecats 6, 7
Pounds/shelters (municipal)
  ferret policy 12, 13
Prednisone for insulinomas 57
Pregnancy
  gestation 41
  nutritional requirement 34, 44, 45
Proglycem for insulinomas 57
Prolapsed rectum 32, 35, 38, 61

Proliferative colitis 35, 38, 51, 61, 62
Protein requirement 44
Public Health Department
  rabies policy 37
Rabies 54, 55, 60
  allergic reaction to vaccine 30
  bats 55
  distinguish from exhuberance 15
  exposure 37, 54, 55
  vaccines 54, 63
  legal status of ferrets 10, 37, 55
  test after bite 10, 37, 55
  transmission 54, 55
  vaccination 10, 30, 37, 54
Respiratory infections 35, 37, 45, 50, 56
  at shows 39
Bordetella bronchiseptica 38, 50
  colds 21, 35, 50
  in baby kits 21
  influenza 35, 37, 50
  treatment 21. 35, 45, 50
  ventilation 38, 50
  when boarded 38
Restraint 29
Rodents 6, 13
Sarcoptic mange 60
  itching 34
Scratching (see Itching) 34
Scruffing
  for nail trimming 29
  to clean ears 28
Shavings 21
Shedding 27, 33, 53
  coat change 27
  effect of seasons 27, 33, 53
  hairballs 27, 52
Shows (see Ferret shows) 39
Sleeping habits 8, 9, 10, 12, 14, 21, 22
Sleeping tubes 8, 21, 22
Slippery floors, injuries 38
Snacks 24, 59
  as training aid 24, 25, 26, 29
  for ferrets with insulinomas 45, 57
Sneezing
  caused by litter 21, 26, 50
  upper respiratory infections 21, 39, 50
Spaying
  benefits 27, 31, 40

effects of   17, 27, 31, 33, 40, 56
kits   10, 17, 56
surgical procedure   31, 59
when to spay   31, 40
Sprites   6
States forbidding ferrets   63
penalties   10
Stool check   21, 30, 47, 51
Straining   51
Stress
air travel   21, 37, 50
hot environment   20, 21, 37, 50, 51
overcrowding   50, 51
poor nutrition   50, 51
travelling   37, 50
upper respiratory infections   20, 35, 38, 39, 50
ventilation   35, 38, 50
wasting diseases   51, 52
weaning   50, 51
Supplements (see nutritional supliments)
wasting diseases   62
Surgery   33, 58
for cancer   56, 57
cesarean section   42
descenting   10, 32
foreign bodies   25, 53
Swollen vulva
adrenal gland tumor   34, 56, 57
Tail alopecia   33
Taurine   43
deficiency   55
Teeth
age of eruption   30, 32, 41
cleaning   30, 32, 33
crooked   32, 42
plaque   24, 30, 31, 33, 44, 59
Temperature
at boarding kennels   38
comfortable for ferrets   20, 22, 35, 51
heat stroke   22, 34, 37
in pet shops   20, 50
Testicles, enlarged (adrenal gland tumors) 56
Toys suitable for ferrets   25
Training
using treats as reward   25, 26
Travelling
exposure to disease   37

precautions   37
Treats (see Snacks)
Ulcers
Helicobacter mustelae   51, 52
Upper respiratory infections   21, 35, 38, 45, 50
air temperature   50, 59
colds   35, 45, 50
influenza   50
Vaccinations   31
Bordetella bronchiseptica   50
distemper   10, 21, 30, 54, 62
for ferret shows   39
rabies   10, 30, 54, 63
Veterinary care   10, 28-36, 47-48, 50-54, 56, 57
Viral diarrhea
at ferret shows   37, 39
carriers   37
Vocalization   9, 41
chuckling   14
screech   15
Vomiting   35, 38, 53
hairballs   35, 53
Wasting diseases   51, 61
dehydration   52
eosinophilic gastroenteritis   52
Helicobacter gastritis/ulcers   51
lymphosarcoma   52, 56
proliferative colitis   51
treatment   51, 52
Water requirement   22, 24, 45, 50, 51
Water bottles
when boarding   21, 38
Wax, in ears   28
Weaning
stress   50, 51
upper respiratory infections   50
Weasels   6, 54
Weight loss
adrenal gland tumors   56, 57
eosinophilic gastroenteritis   52
Helicobacter mustelae gastritis   51
lymphosarcoma   52, 56
proliferative colitis   51
Worms (see Parasites)   47
Yawning when scruffed   28